Miraculous Healing

*Exploring Miraculous Healing in
God's Redemptive Mission*

Max Sturge, MDiv

◆ **FriesenPress**

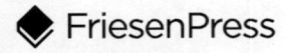

Suite 300 - 990 Fort St
Victoria, BC, Canada, V8V 3K2
www.friesenpress.com

Copyright © 2015 by Max Sturge
Foreword: Major (Dr.) Dawn Howse
First Edition — 2015

All rights reserved.

No part of this publication may be reproduced in any form, or by any means, electronic or mechanical, including photocopying, recording, or any information browsing, storage, or retrieval system, without permission in writing from the publisher.

Unless otherwise stated, all Scriptures are taken from the Holy Bible, New International Version, NIV. Copyright 1973, 1978, 1984 by Biblica, Inc. Used by permission of Zondervan. All rights reserved worldwide. www.zondervan.com. The "NIV" and "New International Version" are trademarks registered in the United States Patent and Trademark Office by Biblica, Inc.

Lyrics for "For This I Have Jesus" by Graham Kendrick: Copyright 1994 Make Way Music, ASCAP (admin. Music Services in the Western Hemisphere) All rights reserved. Used by permission.

ISBN
978-1-4602-7426-2 (Hardcover)
978-1-4602-7427-9 (Paperback)
978-1-4602-7428-6 (eBook)

1. Religion, Biblical Commentary

Distributed to the trade by The Ingram Book Company

Contents

Foreword i
Preface iii
Chapter 1: Looking for Answers 1
Chapter 2: Miracles: Signs With a Purpose 8
Chapter 3: Healing for Israel's Sickness 26
Chapter 4: Heaven On Earth 33
Chapter 5: The Evangelistic Impact of Miraculous Healing 51
Chapter 6: Yes, No, My Grace Is Sufficient 63
Chapter 7: Faith Healing Investigated 73
Chapter 8: The Source of All Healing 82
Chapter 9: How Does God Heal? 94
Chapter 10: Ecstasy and Agony 102
Chapter 11: Increasing Our Capacity for God 113
Chapter 12: God's Pain 124
Endnotes 137

Foreword

Is there really such a thing as a miracle? Can wondrous healings just be explained away by coincidence or science?

In my medical work as a general practitioner, I spend a significant amount of time looking after cancer patients. I marvel daily at the process of healing, and what it really is. In *Miraculous Healing* Max Sturge takes us on a fresh journey through the Bible to examine the history and purposes of God's miraculous interventions. He focuses on miraculous physical healing in the lives of people, particularly—though not exclusively—the descendants of Abraham through whom God promised he would would bless the world (Genesis 12:3), a promise ultimately fulfilled in Jesus Christ.

Why did Jesus perform miracles, particularly physical healings? Couldn't he have just taught and preached? *Miraculous Healing* reminds us that Jesus' ministry and atoning sacrifice fulfill the promise of wholeness and holiness that God had made to his people, Israel, and to the world. In the ministry of Jesus, miraculous healings are signs of God's *redemptive* power. They reveal his love for people, but also point to the time when all sickness and suffering will be obliterated forever.

Are we being petty or selfish when we pray for physical healing? Are there other types of healing that are more important? This book reminds us that God uses miraculous healings as signpost to himself, as well as demonstrations of how the Great Physician alone can provide the healing balm for the ailing soul.

I encourage you to read, share and discuss this book. May our eyes be opened to the awesomeness of our Almighty God who still works to draw us to himself, to heal our brokenness and sometimes interacts redemptively with us in ways that can only be described as miraculous.

G. Dawn Howse, MD
Major (Rtd.)

Preface

Why did I want to write a book about miraculous healing? I've always been a curious, questioning person, looking for answers to life's big questions. I recall, as a young university student, walking across the lawns of Memorial University of Newfoundland and pondering why God allowed war and destruction to snuff out the lives of millions of people. Why so much evil? "Lord, why don't you do something about it?" Then, it dawned on me: The Bible reveals that God came to earth in Jesus Christ his Son to set all things right. If humanity does not co-operate with him, why blame God for the pain we inflict on one another? I later read the Old Testament Book of Habakkuk and discovered that Habakkuk was puzzled by God's seeming lack of action in allowing the wicked Babylonians to inflict so much destruction and suffering upon his own people. Like Habakkuk, I have learned to trust God in perplexing and painful times: "The righteous will live by his faith" (Habakkuk 2:4).

A university course I took on physical anthropology challenged my faith in God as Creator of the universe, including human beings. Again God's Word provided helpful reassurance: "See to it that no one takes you captive through hollow and deceptive philosophy, which depends on human tradition and the basic principles of this world rather than on Christ" (Colossians 2:8). I respect scientific inquiry and appreciate the countless benefits resulting from science. This verse reminded me, however, that science generally and evolution specifically attempt to explain human origins and development exclusively from a naturalistic philosophy of life, thus ignoring the biblical revelation of God the Creator.

Faith in God is neither irrational nor anti-scientific. It is not unreasonable to believe that God created and sustains the universe (Genesis 1:1; John 1:1-3; Colossians 1:15-17; Hebrews 1:1-3). Discovering that many reputable scientists are committed Christians has encouraged my faith over the years, including those who believe in an evolutionary process guided by God. Some Christian scientists believe that God occasionally miraculously heals when human medical knowledge and skill have failed to cure a particular individual.

Finally, I decided to write about miraculous healing because I felt compelled to do so, believing that those who read it will benefit spiritually and in their understanding of God's mission in and purpose for the world. Hopefully, what I share may even be a comfort to people for whom pain and suffering are ongoing personal issues.

My primary focus is exploring miraculous physical healing in the Old and New Testaments, with the overarching theme of how it fits into the unfolding story of God's redemptive plan for the world. I will provide information from a couple of investigations into claims of miraculous healings from more recent years. I also

Preface

will share the profound and—what may be for some readers—surprising significance and purpose of healing in Jesus' ministry, and how his cross and resurrection relate to human pain and suffering. Does God understand our pain? Does he care about our suffering? I invite you to join me in this exciting journey of exploring what the Bible reveals about this fascinating and sometimes controversial topic of miraculous healing. My prayer is that your mind will be enlightened and your heart will be warmed and encouraged.

Chapter 1
Looking for Answers

Pain in various forms has punctuated my life since childhood. I recall begging my mother for a kitten. Scampy became the joy of my life. Unfortunately, she often urinated in our slippers and shoes. Knowing my mother's intolerance of uncleanness, I feared she would put Scampy down for her feline misbehavior. As it turned out, she did not have to execute the cat, even if she wanted to.

While sitting on the front steps of our house on a sunny summer morning, I was unexpectedly ushered into childhood grief. Hearing the screeching of a car's tires, I hurried around the corner of our house and saw Scampy squashed on the gravel road. I ran back into the house and seeing dad's 12-gauge shotgun hanging on the wall, I angrily shouted at mom, "Get dad's gun and shoot the United Church minister. He just ran over and killed Scampy!" Disproportionate vengeance I now admit, but it felt like perfect justice on that day.

On one of his visits to our home, my older sister's boyfriend, Fred Pelley—who later became her husband—brought me three pet rabbits. All three quickly escaped from the pen enclosure that my father had made for them. Did the rabbits escape by digging under the wire meshing? Knowing that I would never see them again saddened me. Later Dad bought a young horse, Star, to haul firewood home on a sled in the winter. I enjoyed listening to the Lone Ranger and Tonto program on radio, and later loved watching them in movies and on television. I dreamed of a day when I would be old enough to ride Star the way the Lone Ranger rode his horse, Silver. My dream was shattered one day when I saw white froth on the sides of Star's mouth. My heart sank when my father told me that our young horse would have to be led over the marsh, where he would be shot and buried to put him out of his misery. Should I have prayed for my lost rabbits to return home and for God to heal Star?

More seriously, when I was six years old a persistent lung ailment resulted in my being hospitalized for six months. If my parents had not taken me from the small hospital near our home town of Wesleyville (now New-Wes-Valley), N.L., and had me transferred to the General Hospital in St. John's, I may have died. My lung ailment reoccurred when I was twelve and doctors hospitalized me again. Three months passed before they concluded I was permanently cured. Loneliness was an unwelcome companion during these prolonged stays in hospital. I learned years later that my family and relatives had prayed for my recovery. Did God have a purpose for these lengthy periods of illness?

Just before my teenage years, my devout grandmother lived with us for a while. During that time, when she was 73, she came down with bowel cancer and died. I do not recall either my family or our church congregation praying for her healing. I do not think it occurred to us to do so. We just assumed it was her time to go.

Should we have prayed for her to get well? Or, when a person reaches a certain age, should we pray for a miraculous cure of a terminal illness? Should any prayer for the healing of the sick or dying include the proviso, "Lord, if it is your will?"

In my mid-twenties, hay fever afflicted me severely. Without antihistamines, I sneezed endlessly, and without eye drops, the itching was unbearable. Even with the use of drugs, I experienced several frustrating weeks every spring—and still do. I wondered about praying to God for healing, but I could not decide if I should bother him about my ailment. With so many people seriously ill and others trying to cope with incessant pain, was I being a bit frivolous in wanting to be delivered from hay fever? Did God want me to learn some valuable truths about life through having to cope with this annoying complaint? Though I eventually prayed for God to heal me, I still have spring hay fever—though not as severe as it used to be. I prayed for patience to become more appreciative of the good health I experienced the rest of the year. Should I still be praying to be cured of hay fever?

In the winter of 2005, I felt I needed to inject an exciting recreational diversion into my weekly pastoral routine. I decided, at the ripe old age of 58, to take up skiing. For seven weeks I skied once a week without incident. On the eighth week I decided to try a different resort. As I was slowing down near the end of my final downhill run, a male skier slammed into my back and drove me face first into the hard snow. I tried to protect myself by putting my arms in front of me, but the force of the collision pushed my right arm back too far and fractured my upper humerus and shoulder in four places. Two collaborating orthopedic surgeons decided against shoulder replacement or any other surgery. Instead, they put my arm in a sling.

At the orthopedic doctor's suggestion, I removed the sling six weeks later and discovered I could not raise my right arm higher than my head. On my next visit to the hospital, the doctor, betraying not the slightest degree of sympathy, announced: "You have a frozen shoulder." Having never heard of such a condition, I was too shocked to ask him what it meant.

After years of several types of therapy, I regained significant mobility. The upper humerus, however, no longer fits properly into its socket, and with so much remaining scar tissue, I will always need to perform daily stretches and exercises to retain right arm and shoulder mobility. In addition to that aggravation I have osteoarthritis in my right hand, shoulder and neck, and a deteriorating disc in my lower back that requires periodic chiropractic adjustments. None of these ailments incapacitates me. However, I can no longer run, jog, golf or ski, and swimming continuously for more than a few minutes becomes painful. You can probably appreciate why miraculous healing appeals to me. Should I pray for God to heal these infirmities?

Some Christians have prayed earnestly for the physical healing of a dying loved one, but to no avail. There are, however, instances when God has seemingly intervened and a terminally ill person has been restored to complete health. Why is one healed and not the other?

We occasionally hear of Christian groups or sects who believe that in response to our faith and prayers, God will heal *any* disease. Some of those religious groups forbid adherents from seeking any type of medical assistance. In some cases, parents have allowed children to die because they believed that faith in God alone would bring the required cure. Is this an appropriate response to illness?

I recall watching a passionate television preacher ask questions such as, "Do you need a miracle? Are we expecting almighty God to perform miracles for us in our church? He can do it, brother! He can do it, sister!" Is miraculous healing simply for the asking? Some preachers' orations give the impression that God is a heavenly chore boy waiting to satisfy our every desire and need. Is life, including the Christian life, that simple?

On the other hand, have we become so scientifically and technologically competent in producing miracles without God's direct intervention (e.g. heart, lung, kidney, womb transplants), that it does not occur to us that he may be able to pull one off without our medical assistance? Or, have we become so entrapped in our theological and scientific presuppositions that we are unable to believe, for example, that God would directly restore a terminally ill person to full health without medical intervention?

Illness and suffering are unavoidable. Some people see widespread suffering as a barrier to believing in a perfectly good and all-powerful God. In the introduction to her book, *A Place of Healing*, quadriplegic Joni Eareckson Tada quotes John Stott: "The fact of suffering undoubtedly constitutes the single greatest challenge to the Christian faith, and has been in every generation." (1)

The entire Book of Job wrestles specifically with the issue of innocent suffering, the suffering of the righteous. Job fired many complaints and questions at God about his calamities. In the end, he did not get any answers—at least not the kinds of answers he wanted. He did, however, receive a profound revelation of the mighty creative power and awesome majesty of God (Job 38-41), which elicited the confession: "My ears have heard of you but now my eyes have seen you. Therefore I...repent in dust and ashes" (Job 42:5-6).

Job's magnificent vision of the incomparable glory of God eliminated his need for an answer to why a righteous person like himself should have to suffer so much. He found comfort in simply realizing that the Creator of the universe was with him.

The issue of human suffering and the question of whether God intervenes to miraculously heal have intrigued me for many years. Some Christians claim that God answered their prayer for a miraculous healing; others are puzzled why God didn't do likewise for them. As you journey with me you will discover—as I have—some satisfying biblical and theological insights into how miraculous healing, pain and suffering fit into the big story line of the Bible and God's plan for humanity. Discovering in Jesus' ministry the connection between his healing miracles and the kingdom of heaven will be enlightening. Understanding them throughout the Bible as 'signs' will help us to discern their purpose in God's redemptive mission in the world. The most profound insight for some readers may be discovering that the Lord God Almighty identifies fully with and shares in their suffering and pain.

Discussion Questions

1. What kinds of pain or suffering have you experienced personally? Have you prayed for God to heal you? Why or why not?

2. Do you have a family member or friend who died at a relatively young age because of a serious illness? Did you or anyone you know ask God to heal them? Why or why not?

3. When a person reaches a certain age, should we pray for a miraculous cure of a terminal illness or any illness? Why or why not?

4. Should any prayer for the healing of the sick or dying include the proviso, "Lord, if it is your will?" Why or why not?

Chapter 2
Miracles: Signs With a Purpose

I did not realize how frequently the word *miracle* is used today—until I began writing this book. You may have watched on television a person who had won $10 million or $50 million in a lottery enthusiastically exclaiming, "I can't believe it. It's a miracle!" A small child falls four stories from an apartment building and survives with only minor bruising. The family and local news media call it a miracle. A National Hockey League team is near the bottom in the standings. No one expects it to make the playoffs. The team goes on an incredible winning streak and ends up winning the coveted Stanley Cup. No one would be surprised to hear a loyal fan saying, "I would have never believed this was possible. It's a miracle!" After witnessing his wife's giving birth, a young father exclaims, "It's a miracle!"

On May 9, 2013, I viewed a television report about a woman in Bangladesh who, for 17 days had been buried with hundreds of others in a tragic accident because the factory where they worked collapsed. Rescuers found her alive. The news broadcaster began with, "A miraculous story out of Bangladesh today." The next day another reporter referred to the lady's survival as a miracle.

A week or so later, a television announcer who was reporting on the devastating tornado that tore through Moore, Oklahoma, USA, and killed 24 people, called his news item "Miracles Beneath the Rubble." Emergency responders eventually pulled scores of survivors from the piles of debris. In the sense of being an awe-inspiring event or an unanticipated, tremendously beneficial occurrence, these examples qualify as a miracle.

None of the rescued individuals or news reports credited God with the miracle. Perhaps some genuinely believed God performed a miracle for them. Though most people believe there is a supreme Being, many nevertheless do not believe that he directly interacts with humans. Some deny the existence of God. Their chosen bias against anything supernatural prohibits belief in divine miracles. Others believe that if God exists, nothing can be known about him, including whether he performs supernatural healing, for example. However, believing in miracles or divine interactions in human affairs is not wishful thinking for those who believe in the Bible's revelation of God's creating heaven and earth out of nothing (Genesis 1:1).

God In Space and Time

The current scientific consensus is that the universe began nearly 14 billion years ago with what scientists call the Big Bang. Before that event nothing existed. Since nothing cannot create anything, it follows that something or someone must have caused the Big Bang. I believe the biblical revelation that God the Father created the universe by his Spirit (Genesis 1:1-2) and through his Son,

Jesus Christ: "In the past God spoke to our forefathers through the prophets at many times and in various ways, but in these last days he has spoken to us by his Son...through whom he created the universe" (Hebrews 1:1-2; see also John 1:1-3; Colossians 1:15-16). God's creating the cosmos out of nothing by his powerful Word is an incredible miracle requiring an act of faith to believe it. The Bible also teaches that "in [Jesus Christ] all things hold together" (Colossians 1:17), meaning that he sustains all of creation. Otherwise the cosmos would collapse into total chaos. The Bible reveals that God ultimately manifested himself in space and time in becoming one of us in Jesus Christ, Emmanuel, God with us (Matthew 1:23), an event that must be called miraculous.

The Bible tells the story of a God who as Creator and Redeemer interacts with his creation. These interactions sometimes result in remarkable occurrences, including physical healing. These healings are not, however, isolated occurrences without any overall purpose. They are, as we will see, an integral part of the Bible's overarching story of God's redemptive mission in the world.

God's Redemptive Mission

After God's judgment upon extreme wickedness through a flood in which only Noah and his family survived (Genesis 6:5; 9:12-16), God wanted to create a new humanity who would bless the world—a holy people who would lovingly obey him and demonstrate a better way of being human than previously shown by the ungodly peoples who perished in the catastrophic flood. He began with an individual. He called Abram (later Abraham), a descendant of Noah, to leave his country and household to go to a land God would show him, promising that through him and his descendants (they later became the nation of Israel) all peoples on earth would be blessed (Genesis 12:1-3). God promised him a son through his wife, Sarai (later Sarah), and reaffirmed the promise many years later when Abraham was 99 years old and his wife was 90 (Genesis 17:1-8, 15-22). But how could this possibly happen at such an advanced age?

Sarah's eventual conception of a son, Isaac, would require divine intervention—a miracle! The purpose of the miracle? In healing Sarah's barrenness, God demonstrated his faithfulness to his promise to Abraham of many descendants who would carry out his mission of blessing the world. God is saying: "The promise can only can be fulfilled through *my* initiative and power and I can be trusted absolutely."

This motif of putting one's faith in God's promise and power for conception in old age or barrenness—in humanly impossible situations—punctuates the biblical story of salvation. The pattern reoccurs in the stories of Isaac and Rebekah for the conception of Jacob and Esau (Genesis 25:19-21). Jacob's name was changed to Israel and his twelve sons became the nation of Israel. The pattern is repeated with Hannah and Elkanah in the birth of Samuel, who anointed Saul as Israel's first king (1 Samuel 1), and the birth of John the Baptizer, the forerunner of Jesus, to Zechariah and Elizabeth (Luke 1:5-25). The motif culminates in the birth of Jesus Christ, a descendant of Abraham, who would become the ultimate 'blessing' as the world's Saviour from the guilt and power of sin.

The Bible says that Mary became pregnant through God the Holy Spirit's direct intervention, resulting in a miracle beyond words to explain. The birth of Jesus Christ, the God-Man (Matthew 1:18; Luke 1:34-35), along with his sinless life, qualified him alone as humankind's Saviour. While his conception is a mystery beyond our understanding, it is nevertheless not irrational or impossible—if we believe in a God with whom nothing is impossible (Luke 1:37). For people who believe that everything can be explained scientifically without reference to God, divine or supernatural explanations are unnecessary. Their beliefs about life and the universe assume divine miracles cannot happen, thus requiring them to look for other explanations. The Bible reveals God acting in history and sometimes in a way that is best described as miraculous.

Miracles As Purposeful 'Signs'

A key to understanding miracles in the Bible is its portrayal of them as signs—though all signs are not miraculous. To accompany his spoken word and vouch for its validity and reliability, God uses signs as his message carriers. After the flood, from which only Noah and his family survived, a rainbow becomes the sign guaranteeing God's promise that he will never again destroy the earth by flooding (Genesis 9:8-17). Before freeing Abraham's descendants, the ancient Hebrews, from slavery in Egypt, God instructed them through Moses to sprinkle the blood of a sacrificial animal on the door frames of their houses. The blood sign vouched for his promise to protect their oldest sons from the death that would strike down all of Egypt's eldest sons (Exodus 12:4-7, 13).

In God's redemptive mission through Abraham's descendants (Israel), miraculous signs are clustered primarily in three critical periods of Israel's history: first, in their salvation from slavery and entry into the Promised Land; second, during the intense conflict with pagan religion (the Baals) associated with the ministries of Elijah and Elisha; and finally, in the time of Daniel when God's people were in exile in Babylon and Israel's God needed to demonstrate his supremacy and the faithfulness of Daniel and his friends.

The Book of Numbers tells the story of Abraham's descendants, the Israelites, wandering in the wilderness after God delivered them from slavery in Egypt through Moses' leadership. At a critical point in the story, Miriam, Moses' sister, and Aaron, his brother, who was the high priest, criticized him for marrying a Cushite woman. They were obviously jealous of Moses' prestigious authority (Numbers 12:1-2) and tried to hide it by focusing on his wife. They were actually challenging his authority to lead his people—even though God had called him to that task—and thus indirectly criticizing God's decision.

How did God defend Moses' authority? He disciplined Miriam by afflicting her with leprosy such that she was "like a stillborn infant coming from its mother's womb with its flesh half eaten away" (Numbers 12:10, 12). A painful sight to behold! Aaron was exempted from discipline—probably because he was the high priest. Also, mentioning Miriam's name in 12:1 before Aaron's likely implies she was the instigator. Aaron begged Moses not to hold this sin against her. Moses then cried out to God to heal his sister and God cured her (Numbers 12:13-15). Only God's direct action could have wrought such a remarkable recovery, thus revealing the purpose of the miracle: to reaffirm Moses as God's chosen servant leader of his people.

To encourage Moses to trust his promise of delivering his people from Egyptian bondage, God declared: "I know that the king of Egypt will not let you go unless a mighty hand compels him. So I will stretch out my hand and strike the Egyptians with all the wonders that I will perform among them. After that, he will let you go" (Exodus 3:19-20). After the pharaoh refused Moses' initial request to free the Israelites, God performed miraculous signs through Moses to try to persuade the pharaoh to change his mind. These signs included the sand of Egypt becoming gnats (Exodus 8:16-19), flies inundating the land (Exodus 8:20-25), the death of all the livestock—except the Israelites' animals (Exodus 9:1-7), and locusts filling all the Egyptians' houses but avoiding the homes of the Israelites. Craig Blomberg asserts that "Not one of the plagues is necessarily supernatural; in fact, their sequence is often scientifically logical. But their timing and geographical limitations point to God's sovereign interventions on Israel's behalf." (1)

Throughout this dramatic story, the text repeatedly tells us the *purpose* of these signs: "I have heard the groaning of the Israelites, whom the Egyptians are enslaving, and I have remembered my covenant. Therefore say to the Israelites: 'I am the LORD, and I will bring you out from under the yoke of the Egyptians…I will redeem you with an outstretched arm and with mighty acts of

Miracles: Signs With a Purpose

judgment. I will take you as my own people. *Then you will know that I am the LORD your God, who brought you out from under the yoke of the Egyptians.* And I will bring you to the land I swore with uplifted hand to give to Abraham, to Isaac and to Jacob' " (Exodus 6:5-8). (Exodus 3:14 says that I AM WHO I AM was the special name God revealed to Moses when he called him to free his people from slavery. Some translations say the LORD, others translate the name as Yahweh.) The LORD declares that "the Egyptians will [also] know that I am the LORD when I stretch out my hand against Egypt and bring the Israelites out of it" (Exodus 7:5; also Exodus 8:22; 9:13-17, 27-30; 10:1-2).

These signs were purposeful in telling God's people they should trust Moses as his chosen servant to free them from slavery. The signs also served to persuade his people and the Egyptians that the Israelites' God—the LORD—was far superior to Egypt's gods and consequently was the one and only true God whom they should worship.

The Egyptian pharaoh finally let the Israelite slaves go, but he and his officials quickly realized they were losing all of their free labor and changed their minds (14:5-9). They cornered the Israelites at the Sea of Reeds (the Red Sea). Unable to escape, the people complained bitterly to Moses that they would have been better off serving the Egyptians (14:10-12). Moses' encouraging response was: "Do not be afraid…The LORD will fight for you; you need only to be still" (14:13-14). In obedience to God's word, Moses held his staff out over the sea. With the assistance of a strong east wind, dry land opened up through the water for them to escape to the other side (14:21-22). The wheels of the

Egyptian chariots came off or became jammed in the muddy soil. At daybreak, when Moses lifted his hand towards the sea, its waters flowed back and engulfed the Egyptian army. None survived (14:23-31). The result? When they "saw the great power the LORD displayed against the Egyptians, *the people [reverenced] the LORD and put their trust in him and in Moses his servant*" (Exodus 14:31).

This miraculous deliverance renewed Israel's faith in the LORD and in Moses, but it did more. Salvation from Egyptian slavery resulted in the initial Passover becoming the annually celebrated redemptive event in Israel's centuries-long history. From a Christian perspective, it is also the great saving event in the Old Testament that anticipates the greater salvation secured by God for the world through his Son, Jesus Christ: "In Christ we have redemption through his blood, the forgiveness of sins" (Ephesians 1:7).

During the Israelites' wanderings in the wilderness, God miraculously provided for their needs through daily manna, quail (Exodus 16:11-18) and water from a rock (17:1-7). God's intention for them through the wilderness experience seemed to be to develop in them a daily dependence on him so that they would trust *him* to meet their needs instead of turning to other gods.

Compromising God's Mission

Before looking at the second appearance of miraculous signs in Israel's history, we need to understand God's expectations of them as his mission people. After rescuing them from Egyptian slavery, he entered into a special covenant with them at Mt. Sinai. They were to "obey [him] fully" and "be for [him] a kingdom of priests and a holy nation" (Exodus 19:5, 6). Priests intercede for people before God. He obviously wants Israel to be his intercessors, to mediate to others the knowledge of him, the LORD, as the one true God and thus become a blessing to all peoples as originally promised to their founding father, Abraham (Genesis 12:3). In becoming a holy priesthood, they would reflect the character of their holy God to the rest of the world. What would that individual and corporate holiness look like?

Included in the covenant God initiated with the Israelites at Mt. Sinai were the Ten Commandments (Exodus 20). Their obedience to these commandments will separate them in many ways from neighbouring nations and thus ensure their holiness before God. In this covenant relationship they can have no other gods, nor make any physical images of him. They must not misuse his name. They are to especially honour God by keeping the seventh day of the week (Sabbath) 'holy'. They are to respect their parents, not murder, commit adultery, steal, give false testimony about their neighbour or covet anything belonging to others (Exodus 20:1-17). These were the foundation stones for God's holy people to become a blessing to others by their individual and corporate behaviour. How faithful were they to their calling and mission? They became chronic covenant violators, especially by incorporating into their worship the idolatrous practices of their neighbours, and thus compromised their calling and mission.

Hundreds of years after the Exodus and wilderness wanderings, a second cluster of miraculous signs appears in the history of

God's mission people. After the reigns of Saul, David and Solomon, God's people divided into two kingdoms: Israel in the north with its capital in Samaria and Judah in the south, with Jerusalem as its seat of power. To discourage Israelites from going to Jerusalem for worship and religious festivals, which could tempt them to return to the southern kingdom of Judah, Jeroboam, the first ruler over the northern kingdom, built idolatrous worship centres in Bethel and Dan in the north. He staffed them with priests from the local population rather than with Levites (1 Kings 12:25-33). These actions blatantly violated the Israelites' covenant with God (sometimes referred to as the Mosaic or Sinai Covenant), which prohibited the worship of idols and restricted the priesthood to the Levites (Exodus 20:1-4; Numbers 3-4).

On one occasion, when King Jeroboam was standing by the altar in Bethel in the northern kingdom of Israel to make an offering, a man of God (prophet) from the southern kingdom of Judah pronounced God's judgment upon the altar, saying that a future king from the south, Josiah, would sacrifice (i.e. kill) the priests who were offering sacrifices in these northern worship centres (1 Kings 13:1-2). Then he gave a sign to vouch for the certainty of this judgment: "The altar will be split apart and the ashes on it will be poured out" (1 Kings 13:3).

Jeroboam had no intention of relinquishing religious and political control over his kingdom. He pointed his hand towards the prophet and angrily ordered his guards to seize him. At that precise moment his hand "shriveled up so that he could not pull it back" (1 Kings 13:4), and the altar split apart and its ashes poured out—the sign the man of God had prophesied (1 Kings 13:5).

Startled, Jeroboam pleaded with the prophet: "Intercede with the LORD your God…that my hand may be restored" (Kings 13:6). The prophet prayed to God for healing and Jeroboam's hand was fully restored to normal functioning (1 Kings 13:6).

What message did this sign carry? Clearly, the prophet's God was the one true God who deserved Jeroboam's exclusive worship. The altar sign and healing resulted in Jeroboam sparing the prophet's life. He gratefully invited the man of God to dine with him and accept a gift, but the prophet declined—probably because he did not want Jeroboam to credit him with the healing and to demonstrate that God's favour cannot be bought (1Kings 13:7-10). Jeroboam never repented, but reigned for twenty-two years. His idolatrous actions influenced succeeding kings of the northern kingdom (Israel) until the Assyrians exiled the Israelites in 721 BC (1 Kings 14:14-16; 2 Kings 17:1-23). Israel's prophets repeatedly stressed that their exile was God's punishment for their covenant violations.

Both 1 and 2 Kings record generations of political instability in the southern kingdom of Judah, and especially in the northern kingdom of Israel. Ambitious Israelites wanting to rule over one or the other of these kingdoms would murder the currently reigning king and his entire family. Why? To ensure none of them nor their descendants would be a threat to the throne. At the same time, rampant idolatry was seriously threatening the distinctiveness of God's people (Exodus 20:3-4), thus compromising their mission of being a blessing to the world (Genesis 12:1-3). Leviticus 20:26 declares: "You are to be holy to me because I, the LORD, am holy, and I have set you apart from the nations to be my own." If they worshiped false gods, how could they fulfill their calling of being a kingdom of priests and a holy people who mediated the knowledge of the one true God to the world (Exodus 19:4-6; 20:3-4; Leviticus 20:26)? Was the LORD, Israel's covenanting God, dead? Was he incapable of preserving his people and their faith?

In the midst of political disorder and compromised spiritual and moral integrity, Elijah appeared on the scene. God empowered him to predict to king Ahab of Israel several years of drought (1 Kings 17:1). Ravens fed Elijah and he raised a Sidonian widow's son from apparent death (1 Kings 17:2-24). *Miracles as signs were message carriers.* What was the message here? The LORD was still the source and sustainer of life, and as the woman confessed to Elijah, "Now I know that you are a man of God and that the word of the LORD from your mouth is truth" (1 Kings 17:24). Also, since Sidon was north of Israel in Phoenicia, Elijah's miraculous ministry in that region signified that Israel's God, the LORD, was not a local deity restricted to the geographical boundaries of Israel. He wanted Abraham's descendants to be his mission people for the world, fulfilling the promise first made to Abraham: "I will make you into a great nation...and all peoples on earth will be blessed through you (Genesis 12:3).

A Dramatic Confrontation

This mission theme continues in the spectacular showdown on Mount Carmel where Elijah challenged to a test the 450 prophets of Baal, their god of human and crop fertility, and 400 prophets of Asherah, the goddess of the sea. The false prophets would build an altar on which to place a sacrificial bull. "Then you will call on the name of your god, and I will call on the name of the LORD," said Elijah. "The god who answers by fire—he is God" (1 Kings 18:24). The pagan prophets prayed and danced all day to their god, Baal, but nothing happened, except their frenzied dancing seemed to damage the wooden altar.

Elijah rebuilt the altar. He then placed his carved bull on it and ramped up the odds against himself and God by having the people drench the altar and the offering three times with water (1 Kings 18:30-35). "Answer me, O LORD, answer me, *so these people will know that you, O LORD, are God,* and that you are turning their hearts back again" (1 Kings 18:37), he cried out to God. The result? "Then the fire of the LORD fell and burned up the sacrifice, the wood, the stones and the soil, and also licked up the water in the trench" (1 Kings 18:38). How did the people respond? "They fell prostrate, exclaiming, "The LORD—he is God! The LORD—he is God (v. 39)!" Compared to the LORD's demonstrated fire power, Baal was powerless—no true god at all! The LORD's intervention confirmed him alone as the one supreme God and helped to keep alive the flame of Israel's flickering faith.

A Public Confession of Faith

Elijah's successor, Elisha, likewise performed miracles during this period. He restored to life the dead son of a Shunammite woman in Israel (2 Kings 4:8-37) and healed leprous Naaman, who lived in neighboring Aram (2 Kings 5). Because my major focus will be miraculous physical healing, reflecting upon the narrative about

Miraculous Healing

Naaman provides insights into why Israel's theological historians felt it important to make Naaman's story a part of their journey as God's holy, mission people for the world. Naaman held the powerful position of commander of the army of the king of Aram (Syria today), which bordered Israel on the northeast. The king highly regarded him as a courageous soldier and successful military leader. Interestingly, the text attributes Naaman's success to "the LORD" (2 Kings 5:1), meaning Israel's God.

Unfortunately, Naaman now has leprosy (Hansen's disease). Consequently, his career is on the line because this dreaded disease would prevent him from socializing with other people, including the king. Providentially, Naaman's wife had a young Israelite maid who had been taken captive when Aram and Israel were enemies—as they often were (2 Kings 5:2). She tells Naaman's wife about an Israelite prophet in Samaria who could cure her husband, undoubtedly inspiring hope in an otherwise hopeless situation. This Israelite girl had been taken from her loved ones in an earlier military skirmish, perhaps even by commander Naaman. Why did she even care about him?

The king heeded the girl's advice. He gave Naaman an introductory letter for the king of Israel (perhaps Jehoram, 2 Kings 3:1) along with about 750 pounds (340 kilograms) of silver and about 150 pounds (70 kilograms) of gold, amounting to several million dollars in today's currency! "With this letter I am sending my servant Naaman to you so that you may cure him of leprosy," said the king (2 Kings 5:6). The king of Israel understands the request as the king of Aram expecting *him* to heal Naaman, a task he believes only God can perform. With their history of military conflicts, he's suspicious that the king is trying to manufacture an excuse to pick a fight with him (2 Kings 5:7).

Elisha, God's prophetic messenger, hears about the king of Israel's consternation and invites him to send Naaman to him. Naaman and his entourage arrive at Elisha's house with their horses, chariots, gold and silver. And who greets them? Not Elisha, but his lowly servant, who tells Naaman that to be "restored" and "cleansed" (2 Kings 5:9-10) he must wash seven times in the Jordan River. Naaman felt insulted, likely thinking, "I'm the top general of the Syrian army, and you want *me* to wash in your tiny, muddy Jordan River?" He expects a theatrical demonstration and angrily responds: "I thought that [Elisha] would surely come out to me and stand and call on the name of the LORD his God, wave his hand over the spot and cure me of my leprosy. Are not Abana and Pharpar, the rivers of Damascus better than any of the rivers of Israel? Couldn't I wash in them and be cleansed? So he...went off in a rage" (2 Kings 5:11-12)?

Naaman needed to learn that money and one's high position in society cannot buy healing from the God of Israel. Healing will require obedient faith in and humble obedience to God's Word which, in this case, meant being washed and cleansed in the waters of Israel's little Jordan River. Would Naaman recognize that he needed a humble heart and obedience to God—spiritual healing—more than physical healing? Would he humble himself or would pride be his undoing? Would this powerful military leader publicly confess faith in the LORD, Israel's God? Will he choose life or death?

Understanding Naaman' arrogant mindset, his servants challenged him: "My father, if the prophet had told you to do some great thing, would you not have done it? How much more, then, when he tells you, 'Wash and be cleansed' " (2 Kings 5:13)! Naaman relented and dipped himself seven times in the Jordan. "His flesh was restored and became clean like that of a young boy" (2 Kings 5:14).

Naaman's faith confession highlights the larger purpose of this healing sign: *"Now I know that there is no God in all the world except in Israel"* (2 Kings 5:15). When so many of God's people were being seduced by the idolatrous practices of their neighbors, here is an esteemed pagan leader confessing that "There is no God in all the world except in Israel!"

Profoundly grateful for his new faith and healing, Naaman offered Elisha a gift. The man of God refused to accept it, probably because he wanted to make sure that Naaman would credit God alone and not him for the healing. Secondly, Elisha wanted seared upon Naaman's heart the truth that the God of Israel is the God of all peoples, a God of grace, mercy and compassion who cares for everyone, including Israel's enemies. His favour is undeserving and can never be earned or bought—truths that ancient Israel's theological story tellers stressed to remind her of her divine calling and mission: to be a blessing to the world, to be "a kingdom of priests and a holy nation" who mediated the knowledge of the one true, holy and compassionate God to the world (Genesis 12:3; Exodus 19:5).

In the biblical narrative, healings have a larger purpose than alleviating the suffering of an individual: *healings are message carriers*. They point beyond themselves, revealing something about the character and purposes of God and his mission in the world through Israel. However, as we shall see, a serious spiritual illness continually compromised Israel's mission effectiveness.

Discussion Questions

1. Why are biblical miracles called signs?

2. Why do you think miraculous signs were relatively rare in the history of Israel?

3. What purpose did miraculous signs serve in the Old Testament?

4. Have you ever experienced a 'sign' from God that led to faith or confirmed your faith in him?

Chapter 3
Healing for Israel's Sickness

The Old Testament, including Israel's Wisdom Literature, frequently utilizes the image of physical healing for the healing of the soul for individuals and for people as a whole. David cried out: "Be merciful to me, LORD, for I am faint; O LORD, heal me, for my bones are in agony. My soul is in anguish. How long, O LORD, how long" (Psalm 6: 2-3)? Psalm 107 recounts the consequences of Israel's rebellion against God and uses the concept of corporate spiritual healing to describe God's rescuing them from their troubles: "Some became fools through their rebellious ways and suffered afflictions because of their iniquities. They loathed all food and drew near the gates of death. Then they cried to the LORD in their trouble, and he saved them from their distress. He sent forth his word and healed them; he rescued them from the grave" (Psalm 107:17-20).

The author of Proverbs skillfully contrasts the consequences of right and wrong kinds of speech: "Reckless words pierce like a sword, but the tongue of the wise brings healing" (12:18), and "Pleasant words are a honeycomb, sweet to the soul and healing to the bones" (16:24). However, none used the healing metaphor more often and more passionately than the prophets whose recorded messages became part of Israel's sacred literature.

Though the LORD was Israel's healer (Exodus 15:26), physical healings were not common but, like other miraculous events, were concentrated around critical periods of the nation's history when her existence, faith and mission were in jeopardy. What then was God's greatest concern for his people? Through his spokespersons, the prophets, God revealed that he was deeply concerned about the healing of the entire nation. Why? Because a serious spiritual illness continually compromised Israel's mission effectiveness in being a light to the world, in mediating the knowledge of the one true God to others. Just as a sick doctor cannot carry out his responsibility of providing medical care to others, so Israel's chronic sinfulness, the ongoing violations of her special covenant with God, compromised her ability to be holy and true to her divine calling.

Isaiah often uses personal physical illness as a metaphor to reveal to God's people their moral sickness of heart and soul: "Ah, sinful nation, a people loaded with guilt, a brood of evil doers… They have forsaken the LORD…Why do you persist in rebellion? Your whole head is injured, your whole heart afflicted. From the sole of your foot to the top of your head there is no soundness. Only wounds and wilts and open sores, not cleansed or bandaged or soothed with oil" (1:4-6).

A Sad Diagnosis

God is deeply perturbed that his people worship him with their lips, but their hearts are far from him (Isaiah 29:13). Distraught that his fellow Israelites do not see that mere religious ritualism does not make them the holy, mission people of God, Isaiah announces the approach of a day of national spiritual healing for his people: "In that day the deaf will hear the words of the scroll, and out of gloom and darkness the eyes of the blind will see" (29:18). The deafness and blindness are clearly spiritual in nature.

Jeremiah is equally incisive in diagnosing both his people's and his own spiritual condition: "The heart is deceitful above all things and beyond cure. Who can understand it?...Heal me, O LORD, and I will be healed; save me, and I will be saved, for you are the one I praise" (Jeremiah 17:9, 14). Israel's heart eventually becomes so diseased that God decides to perform a heart transplant on them: "I will cleanse you from all your impurities and from all your idols. I will give you a new heart and put a new spirit in you; I will remove...your heart of stone and give you a heart of flesh" (Ezekiel 36:25-26).

God's people in the southern kingdom of Judah had been devastated by the Babylonian armies and many had already been exiled to Babylon. Jeremiah uses medical imagery in diagnosing his people's spiritual condition: "This is what the LORD says: 'Your wound is incurable, your injury beyond healing. There is no one to plead your cause, no remedy for your sore, no healing for you. All your allies have forgotten you.... Why do you cry over your wound, your pain that has no cure? Because of your great guilt and many sins I have done these things to you' " (Jeremiah 30:12-15). His diagnosis sounds like an incurable form of cancer with doctors concluding, "We can't do anything for you." Israel's corporate disease seems to be a terminal spiritual cancer; a sad diagnosis indeed.

Hope For Spiritual Healing

Are God's mission people beyond redemption? "I will restore you to health and heal your wounds" (Jeremiah 30:17), God promises. There is still hope for the ailing patient. Jeremiah repeats this promise of healing: "I will slay in my anger and wrath. I will hide my face from this city (Jerusalem) because of all its wickedness. Nevertheless, I will bring health and healing to it; I will heal my people and let them enjoy abundant peace and security. I will bring [them] back from captivity.... I will cleanse them from all the sins they have committed against me" (Jeremiah 33:5-8). Back home and recovering from exile in Babylon, God's people are nurtured by their hymns: "The LORD builds up Jerusalem; he gathers the exiles of Israel. He heals the brokenhearted and binds up their wounds" (Psalm 147:2-3).

What is the cure for their spiritual diseases of idolatry, moral laxity and social injustice (Amos 2:4-8; 5:4-13)? What is the prescription for this deadly corporate sickness? Several times in childhood, I developed pneumonia. The pink liquid penicillin the doctor prescribed tasted awful. The only way my mother could get me to swallow it was to mix it with jam and to keep telling me, "It will make you better." God's messenger, Hosea, had earlier pleaded with his people to swallow the bitter medicine of repentance and trust God's healing. Identifying with his people, Hosea exhorts them: "Come, let us return to the LORD. He has torn us to pieces but he will heal us; he has injured us but he will bind up our wounds.... Return, O Israel, to the LORD your God. Your sins have been your downfall.... I will heal their waywardness and love them freely" (Hosea 6:1; 14:1, 4). Many other references show how extensively the prophets utilized this metaphor of physical sickness and the need for spiritual healing to depict Israel's defective relationship with God (Isaiah 6:10; 30:26; Jeremiah 8:15, 22; 14:19; 46:11; 51:8, 9; Hosea 11:3; Ezekiel 34:4).

A Promise of Physical Healing?

To a people who fear that God may not liberate them from captivity in Babylon and restore them to himself and to their homeland, Isaiah proclaims the exciting hope of a brighter tomorrow: "Your God will come.... Then will the eyes of the blind be opened and the ears of the deaf unstopped. Then will the lame leap like a deer, and the tongue of the mute shout for joy" (35:4-6). Is this a promise of miraculous healing from *physical* blindness and deafness? Given the historical situation of Israel's exile, the nation's history of spiritual waywardness and the poetic language of the passage (35:1-2, 6-7), a symbolic interpretation best suits the immediate context. Elsewhere, Isaiah uses the physical disabilities of being blind, deaf, lame and mute to metaphorically describe the spiritual impairments of his servant, the people of Israel (Isaiah 29:15-19; 42:14-20). He bluntly diagnoses their spiritual condition: "Lead out [from Babylonian captivity] those who have eyes but are blind, who have ears but are deaf" (Isaiah 43:8).

Isaiah is saying that Israel has been blind and deaf to the instructions in their covenant with God, ignoring guidance from his prophetic messengers. They have been lame, not walking in the ways of God. Consequently, they experienced the judgment of God in the destruction of their holy temple and nation and in being exiled to Babylon. Now God is promising that he will heal their waywardness and disobedience; he will enable them to walk uprightly before him. In short, he will heal them spiritually.

With Isaiah's confidence in God's absolute sovereignty and believing in God's rule over all nations and all of life, we should not be surprised that this inspired vision of a future healed people would involve their complete wholeness, an end times hope that would include physical as well as spiritual healing. Isaiah's later vision of a "new heavens and a new earth" (Isaiah 65:17) no longer includes the death of infants and everyone lives to old age: "He who fails to reach a hundred will be considered accursed" (Isaiah 65:20). When would all of these things happen? In the New Testament, the Gospel of Luke applies to the healing ministry of Jesus a literal as well as a spiritual fulfillment to Isaiah's promise (see Luke 7:20-22).

Radical Surgery Required

In summary, miraculous physical healing was infrequent in Israel's long history. God's passionate concern was for the corporate, spiritual well-being of his people. Like many of Israel's kings, most were unfaithful to their covenant with God, a covenant their ancestors had entered into at Mount Sinai (Exodus 19-20) and handed down to succeeding generations (Deuteronomy 5:1-3). Their rebellious, stubborn hearts required radical surgery, resulting in a profound inner transformation and reorientation.

How could a spiritually sick people fulfill their calling of being God's model society that would attract other nations to him? Israel needed healing! The prophetic hope was that God would someday heal their waywardness and keep his promise that Abraham and his descendants would fulfill their mission of becoming a blessing to the world (Genesis 12:1-3). The dream was that Israel would be a "kingdom of priests and a holy nation" (Exodus 19:4-6) who would attract Gentiles into embracing the faith of Israel: "I, the LORD, have called you in righteousness; I will take hold of your hand. I will keep you and make you to be a covenant for the people and a light for the Gentiles" (Isaiah 42:6). One day God's kingly rule, the kingdom of heaven, would invade history and transpose life into a higher key. But how would this happen? As we shall see, the arrival on planet Earth of Jesus, Son of God and son of Mary, would answer that question.

Discussion Questions

1. What seemed to be the persistent sickness of Israel, God's mission people? What were the symptoms?

2. In what ways can we be blind, deaf and lame like God's ancient covenant people? How can we best avoid such an illness?

Chapter 4
Heaven On Earth

Old Testament miraculous signs backed up the faith of Israel and also anticipated another intensified period of signs: the incarnation of Jesus, his miracles (including healing), death, resurrection and ascension—which made salvation available not just to Israelites but to the world (John 3:16). In continuity with the Old Testament's revelation of God's interactions in human history, the first book of the New Testament begins: "A record of the genealogy of Jesus Christ the son of David, the son of Abraham" (Matthew 1:1). Mary's conception of Jesus through the power of the Holy Spirit can only be understood as miraculous. "This is how the birth of Jesus Christ came about: His mother Mary was pledged to be married to Joseph, but before they came together, she was found to be with child through the Holy Spirit" (Matthew 1:18).

Luke's account is even more explicit than Matthew's regarding the supernatural nature of Jesus' conception. Responding to the angel's astounding announcement to Mary that she "will be with child and give birth to a son" (Luke 1:31) without sexual relations with her future husband, Joseph, Mary asks incredulously: "How will this be…since I am a virgin" (Luke 1:34)? The response? "The

Holy Spirit will come upon you, and the power of the Most High will overshadow you. So the holy one to be born will be called the Son of God" (Luke 1:35).

The Kingdom of Heaven Arrives

After beginning his public ministry Jesus chose twelve disciples (later called apostles), healed numerous people (Matthew 8-9), and commissioned his disciples to go and "preach this message: 'The kingdom of heaven is near. Heal the sick, raise the dead, cleanse those who have leprosy, drive out demons' " (Matthew 10:1, 7-8). In short, Jesus empowered them to do what he was doing: preaching and demonstrating through miraculous healings that the kingdom of heaven had arrived on earth in and through him.

Does it surprise you to know that New Testament scholars say that the distinguishing mark of Jesus' miracles, including physical healing, is their *end time reference?* In other words, the coming of Jesus and his earthly ministry fulfill God's promises in the Old Testament of a 'Day of the LORD', a future end time when he would pour out his Spirit upon his people (Joel 2:28-32; Acts 2:17-21), when the kingdom of heaven would arrive on earth. God would give his people a new spirit and a new heart (Ezekiel 36:25-26), open the eyes of the blind and the ears of the deaf (Isaiah 35:4-5), and usher in a new world order of peace and justice (Isaiah 2:1-4; 11:1-9).

When John the Baptist, Jesus' cousin and forerunner, was imprisoned and heard of Jesus' ministry, he sent two of his disciples to determine if Jesus was the long-awaited "one who was to come" (Luke 7:19), that is, the Messiah, God's agent to bring his kingly rule to Israel and the world. They found Jesus and asked, "Are you the one who was to come or should we expect someone else" (Luke 7:20)? Quoting Isaiah's prophetic promise, Jesus' response is profoundly significant: "Go back and report to John what you have seen and heard: 'The blind receive sight, the lame walk, those who have leprosy are cured, the deaf hear, the dead are raised, and the good news is preached to the poor' " (Luke 7:21-23; Isaiah 35:5-6; 42:7). Jesus was saying that the hope of messianic salvation was dawning in him.

Healings: Movie Clip Previews

We saw in the Old Testament that miraculous signs were purposeful rather than arbitrary. In the case of Moses, for example, they were an integral part of God's redemptive mission in authenticating Moses as God's true servant to free his people from slavery. They also helped to persuade the Israelites and even some Egyptians that the LORD was the one and only supreme God. *Miraculous signs made visible God's power to save and heal his people.* This idea is made visible in the four gospels that record the coming of Jesus as Saviour of Israel and the world.

The Gospels—Matthew, Mark, Luke and John—show God acting dramatically in miraculous signs through Jesus. However, if people were to grasp the message the signs contained about him and his actions, they would need open hearts and minds towards him and his message. This means that it is through faith that people interpret a particular event as a sign from God, a truth powerfully demonstrated in Jesus' driving demons out of people.

On one occasion people brought to Jesus "a demon-possessed man who was blind and mute, and Jesus healed him, so that he could both talk and see" (Matthew 12:22). This event evoked two opposite responses: "All the people were astonished and said, 'Could this be the Son of David' " (Matthew 12:23)? The common people were beginning to seriously view Jesus as the long-awaited kingly messiah. When the Pharisees, an influential religious group in Israel, heard messiahship being attributed to Jesus, they accused him of casting out demons "by Beelzebub, the prince of demons" (Matthew 12:24).

Why did most people see Jesus' powerful healing miracles as demonstrations of God's sovereign, kingly powers, whereas the deeply religious Pharisees saw them as Satanic in origin? One group had receptive minds to this new thing God was doing, while the religious leaders felt threatened by Jesus' healing miracles and authoritative teachings. Israel was under the control of the Roman emperor. Previous false messiahs had foolishly attempted to lead the people to rebel against Rome, only to be crushed and punished. The Pharisees likely assumed that Jesus, using his charisma and incredible powers, would also lead a revolt and meet the same fate as others before him. They therefore tried to discredit the divine power behind his miracles and thus discourage people from following him.

Their slanderous accusations did not, however, deter Jesus from his teaching and healing mission. He healed the demon-possessed daughter of a Canaanite woman in the Gentile region of Tyre and Sidon (Matthew 15:21-28), demonstrating that God's love embraced all peoples, not just Israelites. As he approached Jericho, in Israel, he healed a blind man who was begging by the side of the road (Luke 18:35-42). Jesus' healing miracles were signs that the kingdom of heaven had dawned in him and his ministry. But what had apparently puzzled John the Baptist and others was that nothing had changed politically. The Romans still oppressively ruled over them. Could Jesus really be the long awaited national deliverer they had anticipated (Isaiah 2:1-5; 11:1-5; 24:21-23; 25)?

Two things Israel would fail to perceive: God's saving rule would not come by force; Jesus' first coming would inaugurate a kingdom of "righteousness, peace and joy in the Holy Spirit" (Romans 14:17). People would enter this spiritual kingdom through repentance and faith in Jesus (Mark 1:15-18). Theologians refer to it as the *already* aspect of the kingdom of heaven on earth. Secondly, Jesus will return (the Second Coming) at an indefinite time in the future to consummate the kingdom, that is, to finish the job he began at his first coming (Revelation 11:15). That is the *not yet* manifestation of God's kingly authority.

"Jesus' words and works are the beginning of the age of salvation, and *the miracles are a foreshadowing and a promise of the coming (future) universal redemption*," explains O. Hofius. "Thus the casting out of demons signals God's invasion into the realm of Satan and its final annihilation (Matthew 12:28-29; Mark 3:20-27; Luke 11:21-22; John 12:31; Revelation 20:1-10); the raising of Jairus' daughter and Lazarus (Mark 5:35-42; John 11) announces that death will [one day] be forever done away with (Isaiah 25:8; 1 Corinthians 15:26; Revelation 21:4); the healing of the sick bears witness to the [eventual] cessation of all suffering" (Revelation 21:4). (1)

The miracles of Jesus are not just remarkable demonstrations of God's power and compassion; they are *message carriers*, loaded with theological content about the kingdom of heaven, particularly their future orientation. To illustrate this truth, let's elaborate on the raising of Jairus' daughter (Mark 5:21-42). Jairus, a synagogue ruler, fell at the feet of Jesus, desperately pleading for Jesus to heal his dying daughter. On his way to this man's house, Jesus was interrupted by a woman who had suffered from menstrual bleeding for twelve years. After her faith healed her by simply touching the garment of Jesus, several men informed Jairus that his daughter had died. Jesus insisted on proceeding to Jairus' home; he discovered mourners "crying and wailing loudly" (Mark 5:38). He told them the girl was not dead but asleep, presumably meaning that for him, awakening her from death would be as easy as awakening her from sleep. They laughed disbelievingly. In the presence of the child's father and mother, and Peter, James and John, Jesus took the girl by the hand, saying, "Little girl, I say to you, get up" (Mark 5:41)! She instantly stood up and walked around, astonishing those present (Mark 5:42).

Though Jairus and his wife would not have perceived the larger end time meaning of this astounding healing, it is as though Jesus is saying to them: "God cares deeply about your daughter. He is pained by your loss and grief. Isaiah prophesied that 'The Sovereign LORD will swallow up death forever...and will wipe away the tears from all faces' (Isaiah 25:8). I will restore your dead daughter to life and wipe the tears from your eyes *today*; however, as happy as you will be to have your daughter back, she will still eventually die like everyone else. But my bringing her back to life now is also a sign pointing to a future day when 'the Sovereign LORD will swallow up death *forever*.' Yes, forever! So, friends, enjoy life under God's sovereign rule, but with your eyes also on that glorious day when death will be no more."

Victor Shepherd explains the theological significance of Jesus' healing miracles this way: "Because Jesus is God in human flesh, then Jesus' miracles are the *invasion* of God's [saving] rule into human life. They are '*signs' of a perfect rule still to come*, a sort of movie clip preview of what heaven will be like—permanently healed bodies and restored minds. Jesus' miracles are thus *pointers* towards God's total healing of creation in the future when [he] returns." (2)

The Primary Purpose of Jesus' Mission

Jesus' healing miracles are signs of the arrival of the prophesied end time salvation. However, because they are, as Shepherd says, "a sort of movie clip preview of what heaven will be like—permanently healed bodies and restored minds"—physical healing, though important, does not become the top priority of Jesus' short ministry. Matthew states that Jesus' purpose was to "save his people from their sins" (Matthew 1:21). Luke reports him as saying that his mission was "to seek and to save the lost" (Luke 19:10). John says that his mission was to make us "children of God" (John 1:12) and to offer eternal life to the world (John 3:16). Like the ministry of the Old Testament prophets we examined earlier, Jesus' priority is spiritual healing—restoring people to a right relationship with God in the now. In short, the initial manifestation of the kingdom of heaven in Jesus' first coming will be followed by a final manifestation—the consummation of the kingdom—at his Second Coming.

Jesus declares at the outset of his public ministry, "The time has come.... The kingdom of God (heaven) is near. Repent and believe the good news" (Mark 1:15). The rest of Mark's gospel reflects the same emphasis. Jesus recruits Simon and his brother, Andrew, to assist him in his early Galilean ministry. What would be their primary responsibility? "Come, follow me...and I will make you fishers of men" (Mark 1:17)!

Though physical healing is not initially stated as part of their mandate, it nevertheless became an integral component of Jesus' holistic ministry. He goes to the synagogue on the Sabbath "to teach" (Mark 1:21). He heals a man "possessed by an evil spirit" (Mark 1:23), and the onlookers are astounded at his new teaching and authority. Shortly thereafter he goes to the home of Simon and Andrew and heals Simon's mother-in-law of a fever. After sunset on the same day, "the whole town gathered at the door and Jesus healed many who had various diseases" (Mark 1:33-34). Jesus was quickly becoming a popular miracle healer in upper Galilee. Was he happy about that perception of his mission? Should physical healing be his primary focus?

Reaffirming Mission Priority

I believe Mark 1:35-39 reveals Jesus deliberately reaffirming his mission focus during this crisis of priorities. After a hectic evening of healings and exorcisms, Jesus got up very early the next morning to find a solitary place to reflect and pray (Mark 1:35)—his typical response when facing a critical decision. "The crisis is the shallow and superficial response of the people to Jesus," asserts Walter Wessell. "[The people] are only interested in what he can do to heal their physical afflictions. So Jesus seeks the strength that only communion and fellowship with the Father can provide." (3)

The disciples appear to have been excited by the size of the crowds. Simon and his companions went to hunt for Jesus, and when they located him they exclaimed, "Everyone is looking for you" (1:37)! The verb that Mark uses for "look for" literally means to track down and hunt, and usually has a hostile sense. The disciples seem to be presuming that Jesus will be delighted to discover that everyone was looking for him and are annoyed at his withdrawal from the crowds. They do not sense that "this popular and shallow reception of him was the very reason he withdrew to pray." (4)

How did Jesus react? "Let us go somewhere else—to the nearby villages—so I can *preach* there also. That is why I have come" (Mark 1:38). The Gospel of Luke succinctly quotes Jesus' purpose: "The Son of Man came to seek and save what was lost" (19:10). Jesus' parables of the lost coin, the lost sheep and the two lost sons recorded in Luke 15 had earlier implied the same purpose. Matthew is equally straightforward: "The Son of Man did not come to be served, but to serve, and to give his life as a ransom for many" (20:28), echoing the sacrificial, atonement theme of Isaiah, who declared: "We all, like sheep, have gone astray...and the Lord has laid on him the iniquity of us all.... He poured out his life unto death, and was numbered with the transgressors. For he bore the sin of many and made intercession for the transgressors" (53:6, 12).

Time alone with the Father in prayer had enabled Jesus to stay on his redemptive course. "Jesus' reply showed that he feared his healings and exorcisms were hindrances to understanding who he really was," says Walter Wessell. "His coming into the world was more to proclaim God's Good News and all that was involved in discipleship and suffering than to be a popular miracle worker. Healings and exorcisms had their place (Mark 1:34, 38-39), but they were not to usurp the primary purpose for which Jesus had come." (5) Luke's emphasis in this incident is on the people's looking for Jesus and trying to keep him in Capernaum performing miraculous healings; however, Luke reiterates Jesus' mission priority of preaching "the good news of the kingdom of God (heaven)" and of the need to present it to a wider audience (Luke 4:42-44).

The Gospel of John is explicit regarding Jesus' concern about people not perceiving the deeper spiritual significance of his mission and the true nature of the kingdom of heaven: "A great crowd of people followed him because they saw the miraculous signs he had performed on the sick" (John 6:2). After his miraculous sign of feeding 5,000 people, "Jesus, knowing that they intended to come and make him king by force, withdrew again to a mountain by himself" (John 6:15).

Jesus refused to be a king who would lead Israel in militarily overthrowing Rome's rule over them and restoring the kind of political glory the nation had experienced centuries earlier under

David and Solomon. When we later hear Jesus saying to Pilate, the Roman governor of Judea stationed in Jerusalem, that his kingdom "is not of this world" (John 18:36), we realize Jesus is rejecting again the kingdom Satan offered him earlier in his ministry (Matthew 4:8-11).

Jesus' mission was not to be a 'bread' or a militaristic messiah, but to "save his people from their sins" (Matthew 1:21) and to offer them eternal life (John 20:30-31). This truth explains why Jesus singled out only one person for healing by the Pool of Bethesda—though there were a lot of disabled people there (John 5:1-9). He cured the centurion's servant without even seeing him (Matthew 8:5-13). Could he have healed every sick person in Palestine? Yes, but that was not going to happen in the initial manifestation of the kingdom of heaven on earth. Physical healing was not Jesus' highest priority during his earthly ministry.

"[People's] illnesses weren't Jesus' focus—the gospel was," comment quadriplegic Joni Eareckson Tada and Steve Estes. "His miracles were a backdrop, a visual aid, to his urgent message. That message was: Sin will kill you, hell is real, God is merciful, his kingdom will change you…. Whenever people missed the point—whenever the immediate benefit of his miracles distracted them from eternal things—the Saviour backed away." (6)

Wanting to extend his mission, Jesus sends out his 12 disciples two by two, and gives them "authority over evil spirits" (Mark 6:7). The result was that "they drove out many demons and anointed many sick people with oil and healed them" (Mark 6:13). But Mark reminds us of the priority of their mission when he says, "They went out and preached that people should repent"

(Mark 6:12), reiterating the mandate Jesus had expressed at the beginning of his ministry: "The time has come.... The kingdom of [heaven] is near. Repent and believe the good news" (1:15).

Post-Resurrection Mission in the Gospels

Matthew's gospel concludes with the resurrected Jesus commissioning his disciples to "make disciples of all nations" (28:19). Luke's focus is not on physical healing but on their responsibility to preach repentance and forgiveness in the power of the Holy Spirit (24:46-49). John emphasizes forgiveness and eternal life (20:21-22, 31). The commissioning at the end of the Gospel of Mark (16:15-18) seems to include physical healing, but with unusual phenomena confirming the truth of the gospel: "And these signs will accompany those who believe: In my name they will drive out demons; they will speak in new tongues; they will pick up snakes with their hands; and when they drink deadly poison, it will not hurt them at all; they will place their hands on sick people and heal them, and they will get well" (Mark 16:17-18).

These verses have spawned snake-handling Christian sects in the United States, including in Florida, Alabama, West Virginia and South Carolina. Ralph Hood, a professor of social psychology and the psychology of religion at the University of Tennessee says there have been more than 100 documented cases of death from serpent (snake) bites in these churches. "In every tradition, people are bitten and maimed by them.... If you go to any [snake-handling church], you'll see people with atrophied hands and missing fingers." (7)

Modern translations of the Bible question the authenticity of Mark 16:9-20, pointing out that the earliest Greek manuscripts used to translate the Bible into English and other languages do not include these verses and believe that the original ending of Mark was lost. They speculate that a later scribe or scribes pieced together material from various sources to create the current ending and thus question the divine inspiration and authority of these verses.

Accepting these verses as they are, the commentary notes on Mark 16:17-18 in *The Life Application Study Bible, New Living Translation* reflect the interpretation of many New Testament scholars: "There are times when God intervenes miraculously to protect his followers. Occasionally he gives them special powers. Paul handles a snake safely (Acts 28:5), and the disciples healed the sick (Matthew 10:1; Acts 3:7-8). This does not mean, however, that we should test God by putting ourselves in dangerous situations or try to tempt the laws of nature. No one should build a religion on a [single] portion of Scripture. God calls us to live as new citizens in the eternal kingdom and to witness by word and service to God's love and power. Our witness should center on Jesus, not on superhero-type stunts." (8)

The Kingdom of Heaven—Already/Not Yet

The fact that after his resurrection Jesus does not promise miraculous physical healing for everyone who asks in faith does not lessen the importance of healings in *his* ministry. "The presence of the messianic, [end time] salvation is...seen in Jesus' miracles of healing, for which the Greek word meaning 'to save' is used" (the same word used for salvation from sin), explains George Eldon Ladd. "...Jesus claimed that [his] deliverances were evidence of the presence of the messianic salvation (Matthew 11:4-5). They were pledges of the life of the end time...kingdom that will [eventually] mean immortality for the body. The kingdom of [heaven] is not only concerned with people's souls, but with the salvation of the whole [person]." (9)

Jesus' healing of the woman who had been suffering from a menstrual hemorrhage supports Ladd's point that salvation encompasses more than deliverance from physical illness. This woman's condition made her ceremonially unclean and therefore unable to worship at the temple in Jerusalem. Since anyone who touched her, they believed, would also become impure and unable to worship at the temple for a while, she must have felt the pain of social isolation, loneliness and shame, perhaps even becoming depressed at times. Probably feeling too embarrassed to encounter Jesus publicly and not wanting to make him ritually unclean, Mark 5:27 says that "she came up behind him in the crowd and touched his robe."

Realizing that power had "gone out from him," Jesus tries to find out who touched him. Why? She wants a physical healing, but Jesus wants more. He is more than a miraculous deliverer from physical ailments. Jesus wants a personal encounter with people. Following Jesus is not only about getting our needs met. It is being in his presence and following him. Meeting Jesus publicly and being freed from her ailment would have also overcome her social isolation. Jesus healed (saved) her socially and physically. O the joy she must have experienced for her *total* healing!

Why didn't Jesus heal all the sick? "The limitation of these physical deliverances illustrates the nature of the present [manifestation of] the kingdom in contrast to its future manifestation," Ladd says. "In the [end time] kingdom, all who are accounted worthy to attain to that age (Luke 20:35) will be saved from sickness and death in the...resurrection. In the *present* working of the kingdom...not all the sick and crippled were saved, nor were all the dead raised.... The miracles of healing...were not an end in themselves. They did not constitute the highest good of the messianic salvation. This fact is illustrated by the arrangement of the phrases in Matthew 11:4-5. Greater than deliverance of the blind and the lame, the lepers and the deaf, even than raising the dead, was the preaching of the good news to the poor. This 'gospel' was the very presence of Jesus himself, and the joy and fellowship that he brought to the poor." (10)

Healings—Making the Kingdom of Heaven Visible

Jesus' priority of spiritual salvation reflects the same emphasis we saw in the Old Testament prophets in expressing the need for a radical heart transformation of the people of God (Jeremiah 33:5-6; Ezekiel 34:4). The God-inspired prophetic dream starts to become a reality in Jesus. That salvation from physical sickness was just the outward aspect of spiritual salvation, Ladd further asserts, is supported in a saying about demon exorcism: "While this miracle was one of the most convincing evidences of the presence of the kingdom [of heaven] (Matthew 12:28; Luke 11:20), [exorcism preceded] God's taking possession of the vacant dwelling. Otherwise, a man is like a house that stands in good order, clean, but empty (Matthew 12:44; Luke 11:24). [Thus physical] healings and exorcisms were the negative side of salvation; the positive side was the incoming of the power and life of God" (11) (see Luke 11:17-21, 24-26). In other words, Jesus was saying that as liberating as it is to have demons removed from one's life, as great as it is to be cleansed from the dirt and mire of the past, unless we are subsequently filled with the Spirit, love and power of God, we will eventually revert to our old life and end up worse off than before.

Jesus' healings were not only expressions of God's saving power and his love for people; they also made the kingdom of heaven visible. Through them Jesus was saying, "Friends, when the kingdom of heaven is fully realized at my return, this is what it will look like to all of my followers: perfect wellness will replace all sickness and pain. No more death, grief and tears." Though salvation from physical diseases and infirmities was an important aspect of Jesus' holistic ministry, physical healing was secondary to the healing of the soul, the healing of people's ruptured relationship with God and with one another.

Renewing Creation

The good news of Jesus' miraculous healings, his atoning death and resurrection, is that in him God has begun the recreation of humankind. God's promise to Abraham that he and his descendants would be a blessing to the world (Genesis 12:3) is fulfilled in Jesus Christ, the son of Abraham. "If anyone is in Christ, he is a new creation. The old has gone, the new has come" (2 Corinthians 5:17) declares the Apostle Paul, former persecutor of the followers of Jesus. Great blessings attend the start-up of God's redemptive reign on earth: forgiveness of sins (Ephesians 1:7), reconciliation with God (2 Corinthians 5:18), the presence of the Holy Spirit in us to strengthen us against temptation, to help us understand God's Word, guide us in our daily decisions (John 14:17, 26; 16:13) and form us into the character likeness of Jesus (Romans 8:29).

These spiritual blessings are the first installment of God's plan to completely heal humanity and all of creation. Greater blessings are yet to follow when he returns—the total healing of those who are in Christ as they receive their immortal, resurrected bodies (1 Corinthians 15:35-57), along with the complete renewal of the cosmos (Romans 8:18-25).

When Adam and Eve sinned, they and all future humankind were subjected to God's curse of "painful toil," "thorns and thistles," increased pain in childbirth and eventually death (Genesis 3:16-19). Paul says that God through Christ will reverse the effects of the fall in nature: "Creation was subject to frustration…but will be liberated from its bondage to decay and brought into the glorious freedom of the children of God" (Romans 8:20-21).

The vision God gave John of that still future fulfillment has inspired and encouraged Christians down through the centuries: "I saw a new heaven and a new earth, for the first heaven and the first earth had passed away.… I saw the Holy City, the new Jerusalem, coming down from God.… I heard a loud voice from the throne saying, 'Now the dwelling of God is with his people, and God himself will be with them.… He will wipe every tear from

Miraculous Healing

their eyes. There will be no more death or mourning or crying or pain, for the old order of things has passed away' " (Revelation 21:1-4). This exhilarating news must be shared with the entire world—which is what we will see happening in the Book of Acts.

Discussion Questions

1. What was the evidence that the kingdom of heaven was manifested in the person and ministry of Jesus?

2. Which of Jesus' miracles, if any, do you find the hardest to believe? Why?

3. Why didn't Jesus make miraculous physical healing the number one priority of his ministry?

4. Why didn't Jesus want to be a military leader to free his people from the oppressive rule of the Roman emperor?

Chapter 5
The Evangelistic Impact of Miraculous Healing

After his resurrection Jesus commanded his followers to "make disciples of all nations…and teach them to obey everything I have commanded you" (Matthew 28:19-20). The Book of Acts continues this exciting story, beginning with the the Holy Spirit filling Christ's disciples to equip them to become his witnesses throughout the world (Acts 1:8). Jesus' Great Commission (Matthew 28:19-20) and his promise of empowerment to witness do not include a mandate to heal physical diseases. However, as the church's mission unfolds, miraculous signs often characterize the witness of the apostles, demonstrating that their preaching was a mighty work of God and a continuation of the ministry of Jesus and the new age he had inaugurated. (1)

Continuing the Ministry of Jesus

Peter healed a man who had been crippled from birth (Acts 3:1-10, 16). This incident and the fearless preaching of Peter and John resulted in the religious authorities jailing them overnight. The next day they appeared before the Sanhedrin, the Jewish religious governing council in Jerusalem (4:1-13). The Sanhedrin realized, however, that their hands were tied because all of Jerusalem seemed to know that the apostles had performed an "outstanding miracle" (Acts 4:16). Moses' miraculous signs confirmed him as God's appointed agent of deliverance from slavery (Exodus 4:1-17; 14:31). Jesus' healing miracles revealed he was God's Messiah for Israel and the world (Matthew 11:1-6). Now Peter's gift of miraculous healing authenticates his and John's spiritual integrity and the credibility of their message of salvation from the guilt and grip of sin (Acts 4:12-20).

When the Sanhedrin let them go, they met with fellow believers and a prayer meeting ensued. What was their burden? "Now, Lord, consider their threats and enable your servants to speak your word with great boldness" (Acts 4:29). Why did they then add: "Stretch out your hand to heal and perform miraculous signs and wonders through the name of your holy servant, Jesus" (4:30)? They were continuing the earthly ministry of Jesus, but in light of the healing of the crippled man, they would have also recognized healing as validating the truth of the gospel they were courageously proclaiming.

Healing Miracles Generate Faith

Though miracles, including healing miracles, did not compel belief, Scripture testifies that they awakened faith in many: "The apostles performed many miraculous *signs* and wonders among the people.... More and more men and women believed in the Lord (i.e. Jesus) and were added to their numbers" (Acts 5:12, 14).

The Evangelistic Impact of Miraculous Healing

The expansion of the church into Samaria through Philip further illustrates this idea: "When the crowds heard Philip and saw the miraculous *signs* he did, they all paid close attention to what he said" (Acts 8:6), and "many paralytics and cripples were healed" (Acts 8:7).

The evangelistic impact of physical healing is also demonstrated in Peter's healing of the paralytic, Aeneas, who had been bedridden for eight years (Acts 9:33-34). "All those who lived in Lydda and Sharon saw him (i.e. the evidence of his healing) and turned to the Lord" (Acts 9:35). Similarly, at Paphos, on the island of Cyprus, Sergius Paulus, the Roman proconsul "believed" and "was amazed at the teaching about the Lord" (Acts 13:12) after he had witnessed the punitive miracle of temporary blindness inflicted by Paul upon the false prophet, Bar-Jesus.

At Iconium, "the Lord...confirmed the message of his grace by enabling [Paul and Barnabas] to do miraculous signs and wonders" (Acts 14:3). Some Jews nevertheless "refused to believe" in spite of these dramatic phenomena and, in fact, "stirred up the Gentiles and poisoned their minds against the brothers" (Acts 14:2). As we saw in Jesus' ministry (Matthew 12:22-28) and earlier in Acts 4, miraculous signs and wonders do not compel belief in Jesus as Lord and Saviour. Along with the message that accompanied them, the signs and wonders sometimes triggered antagonism and persecution as happened in Iconium.

At a special meeting of the apostles in Jerusalem, Peter argued for the formal recognition of repentant Gentiles in the fellowship of the Church on the basis that God showed his acceptance of them by giving them the Holy Spirit (Acts 15:6-9). However, "the whole assembly became silent as they listened to Barnabas and Paul telling about the miraculous *signs* and wonders God had done among the Gentiles through them" (15:12). Miraculous healing was thus interpreted as God's confirmation of their missionary policy of preaching the gospel to the Gentiles.

Healing Promised for All Now?

Having so far explored in the four gospels and Acts the significance of miraculous healings (signs), it would be helpful to see how other New Testament books and authors view these phenomena. Do any of them promise healing now for any disease through prayer and faith alone? In his letter to the church at Rome, Paul says that Christ had used him to lead "the Gentiles to obey God" by what he had "said and done by the power of signs and miracles" (Romans 15:17-19).

He reminded the Galatian church that was slipping back into Jewish ritual observances that God had given them his Spirit and worked "miracles" among them, not on the basis of their observance of the law, but by their faith in the truth of the liberating gospel (Galatians 3:5). He also reminded the Corinthian believers that "the things that mark an apostle—signs, wonders and miracles—were done among [them] with great perseverance" (2 Corinthians 12:12). In short, miraculous signs backed up his gospel message and helped him win converts.

The author of the *Book of Hebrews* also stresses that God testified to the "great salvation" provided in the gospel by "signs, wonders and various miracles" (Hebrews 2:4). As we saw earlier, physical healing was one of those signs, wonders and miracles. These phenomena authenticated the truths preached by Paul and the other apostles. They witnessed to the divine origin of the gospel and therefore to its supernatural power. Calling them signs meant they were not demonstrations of divine power for their own sake; *signs were God's message carriers,* conveying his revelation that *the prophesied, long-awaited messianic salvation has arrived in and through Jesus.*

This New Testament perspective on signs, wonders and miracles is a continuation of what we saw earlier in the Old Testament. Reminding his people, Israel, of the Exodus, the great redemptive acts of God on their behalf, the author of Deuteronomy asks: "Has any god ever tried to take for himself one nation out of another nation, by testings, by miraculous signs and wonders, by war, by a mighty hand and an outstretched arm, or by great and awesome deeds, like all the things the LORD your God did for you in Egypt before your very eyes" (Deuteronomy 4:34)?

Why did God act so powerfully in the saving event of the Exodus? "You were shown these things so that you might know that the LORD is God; besides him, there is no other" (Deuteronomy 4:35). The idea conveyed is that God's liberating his people from slavery in Egypt, his covenanting with them at Mount Sinai and preserving them throughout their many years of desert wandering, all testify to the LORD's compassion and almighty power for his people's salvation. This redemption theme continues into the New Testament. "Jesus did many other miraculous signs in the presence of his disciples, which are not recorded in this book," declares the apostle John in stating the purpose for writing his gospel. "But these are written that you may believe that Jesus is the Christ, the Son of God, and that by believing you may have [eternal] life in his name" (John 20:30).

Physical Healing Guaranteed Now?

One could get the impression thus far that signs, wonders and miracles, including physical healing, would have always been a powerful reality in the lives and ministry of the apostles. Not so. In the section of Paul's letter to the Corinthians (2 Corinthians 12) where he defends his apostolic authority with the reminder of his ministry among them as characterized by "signs, wonders and miracles," he unapologetically recounts his intense struggle and failure to be healed from a chronic physical ailment.

He had earlier written to the believers in Galatia: "It was because of an illness that I first preached the gospel to you. Even though my illness was a trial to you, you did not treat me with contempt or scorn. Instead you welcomed me as if I were an angel of God, as if I were Christ Jesus himself. What has happened to your joy? I can testify that, if you could have done so, you would have torn out your eyes and given them to me" (Galatians 4:13-15). Something was obviously wrong with Paul's eyes.

In closing this letter Paul says, "See what large letters I use as I write to you with my own hand" (Galatians 6:11). Did he use large letters because of poor eyesight and did that impairment occur on the road to Damascus when he became blind and had to be led into the city (Acts 9:7-9)? Or did Paul experience migraine headaches which affected his eyesight? On one occasion he was stoned

(2 Corinthians 11:25). Did one or more of the rocks thrown at him hit his head, causing a brain injury that subsequently affected his eyesight?

Weakness and Power

Paul believed in God's power to heal, otherwise he would not have pleaded with God three times to cure him (2 Corinthians 12:8). God did not remove his affliction. Why not? Paul did not conclude that his faith was deficient, but that God would be better glorified through his on-going weakness than through a miraculous deliverance from it: "[The Lord] said to me, 'My grace is sufficient for you, for my power is made perfect in weakness.' Therefore I will boast all the more gladly about my weakness, so that Christ's power can rest on me" (2 Corinthians 12:9).

Paul saw his physical limitation as God's way of keeping him from becoming conceited and keeping him trusting totally in Christ for the success of his ministry (2 Corinthians 12:7-10). This perspective is likely shaped by his understanding of the cross where "Christ was crucified in weakness, yet *he lives by God's power*. Likewise we are weak in him, yet *by God's power* we will live with him to serve you" (2 Corinthians 13:4; see also 11:30).

Theological Tension—Already/Not Yet

In the Book of Acts remarkable healings complement the evangelistic thrust of the gospel. As in the four Gospels, these healings reflect phase one, the 'already' aspect of the kingdom of heaven on earth. We see in Paul's ministry the same emphasis on evangelism and the spread of the Christian faith, with "miraculous signs and wonders" sometimes assisting that mission. These supernatural events authenticate the apostles and their message, but they do not compel faith.

Why the long interim between the first manifestation of the kingdom of heaven on earth and its consummation at the Second Coming of Jesus? "The Lord is not slow in keeping his promise [to return], as some understand slowness." says Peter. "He is patient with you, not wanting anyone to perish, but everyone to come to repentance," (2 Peter 3:9). In other words, during the time between Jesus' first and second coming, the church's mission is to populate the kingdom of heaven with converts to Christ. In this present manifestation of God's kingly reign on earth, it is more important to have one's estranged relationship with God healed than to be miraculously delivered from a chronic ailment or terminal illness. Why? Even if physically healed, we still eventually die. What then if we are not right with God?

Paul himself was caught in this end time tension between the *already* and *not yet* dimensions of the kingdom of heaven. His apostolic ministry was, on occasion, characterized by "signs, wonders and miracles" (2 Corinthians 12:12; Romans 15:17-19), thus confirming the *already* nature of the kingdom of heaven, validating its presence in the now. He was nevertheless plagued with a 'thorn in the flesh' from which he could get no lasting relief, thus reflecting the *not yet* stage of the kingdom. Paul is an example of all who commit their lives to Jesus Christ and learn to cope with persistent physical ailments, and thus experience a profound spiritual healing and maturity of the soul.

The Evangelistic Impact of Miraculous Healing

Dr. Paul Brand, a Christian surgeon, devoted many years to the physical rehabilitation of leprosy patients in India. He expresses a perspective on miraculous healing with which most Christians would probably agree: "It would be instructive…to read through the four gospels, comparing Jesus' attention to physical healing… with the energy he devoted to a different category of diseases, those of the soul. Why aren't seminars given, books written and television ministries based on proper techniques for dealing with lust, pride, legalism and hypocrisy? Those four favorite themes of Jesus bear far more weight in the gospels than does divine healing. Does an obsession with one and not the other reveal [misguided] values, an almost pagan obsession with the physical body?" (2)

Special Healing Texts: Matthew 8:16-17, James 5:13-16

Those who contend that Jesus' atoning sacrifice on the cross provides physical healing from any disease in this life—if we have enough faith—often use Matthew 8:16-17 and James 5:13-16 to back up their claim. Matthew affirms Jesus' healing of the sick with a quote from the prophet Isaiah: "He took up our infirmities and carried our diseases" (Matthew 8:17). However, using this text to assert that God provides physical healing now for every disease through faith and prayer overlooks the obvious: Matthew uses the quote from Isaiah 53:4 ("by his wounds we are healed") as a prophetic fulfillment to support the earthly healing ministry of *Jesus*, not as a promise guaranteeing physical healing by faith today for everyone who asks for it.

James 5:15 says that "The prayer offered in faith will make the sick person well." Does this verse guarantee physical healing for anyone we pray for—including ourselves? Other Bible verses indicate that asking "in faith" is not the only condition required for a positive response from God. The Apostle Paul fervently prayed for the healing of his painful affliction. Surely he prayed "in faith." Yet, he did not interpret God's no as being the result of his lack of faith in God's ability to heal him. He saw the divine denial as a way of keeping him humbly dependent upon God and thus as an opportunity to continually experience God's sustaining grace. Being weak in himself, he would discover the surpassing power of Christ to effectively handle his health problem and carry out his ministry in spite of his handicap (2 Corinthians 12:7-10).

Conditional Healing

God's denial of Paul's plea and that of countless other Christians who have prayed for physical healing, including healing of a chronic health issue or a terminal illness, means there must be another condition besides faith in order to experience divine intervention. "This is the assurance we have in approaching God: that if we ask anything *according to his will*, he hears us" (1 John 5:14). The request must be according to the will of God. Paul was not healed because he lacked enough faith, but because it was not God's will to cure him. If physical healing is promised in James 5:15, it will only occur if that is God's will for the individual concerned. The reference to confession of sin in James 5:16 implies the need for repentance and for spiritual healing. Because oil was so commonly used as a physical healing balm (Isaiah 1:6; Psalm 23:5; Luke 10:34), it seems that James is encouraging the use of both medical means and prayer when a Christian becomes ill.

Timothy, Paul's young assistant in the work of the gospel, had to cope with an ongoing stomach disorder and other ailments. Paul's advice to him is interesting: "Stop drinking only water, and use a little wine because of your stomach and your frequent illnesses" (1Timothy 5:23). Was Paul aware that sometimes the water they drank on their missionary travels was contaminated and that using a little wine would be beneficial? He did not advise Timothy to "pray, pray, pray." He did not encourage him to have more faith for his healing. On one of his evangelistic travels Paul "left Trophimus sick in Miletus" (2 Timothy 4:20). Did he pray for God to heal Trophimus? Very Likely. Trophimus obviously did not recover quickly enough or Paul would not have left him in Miletus. Were both he and Trophimus lacking in faith? Not likely. Presumably Paul's years of experience with his own medical issue along with sanctified common sense had taught him that miraculous physical healing is not always available for the asking.

"From the perspective of the New Testament writers, the cross is the basis for all the benefits that accrue to believers," writes D.A. Carson, "but this does not mean that all such benefits can be secured at the present time on demand, any more than we have the right and power to demand our resurrection bodies. The availability of any specific blessing can be determined only by appealing to the overall teaching of Scripture. Modern Christians should avoid the…danger of…[demanding] blessings that may not be ours till the end of the age." (3) In short, expecting God to miraculously heal us of every debilitating and terminal disease now is to ask for something that he has planned for the Second Coming of Jesus. This does not mean, however, that God will never directly heal, as we will see in the next chapter.

Discussion Questions

1. Miraculous signs and wonders did not compel belief in Jesus as Messiah and Saviour. In fact, along with the message that accompanied them, why did they sometimes trigger antagonism and persecution?

2. Why do you think miraculous signs awakened faith in some but not in others?

3. Why did Paul pray for God to cure him of his affliction? Why didn't God heal him?

4. In light of the information in this chapter, how would you interpret Psalm 103:2-3: "Praise the LORD, O my soul, and forget not all his benefits—who forgives all your sins and heals all your diseases?"

Chapter 6

Yes, No, My Grace Is Sufficient

Though miraculous healing is not available today by simply asking God for it, does that mean we can never expect a person with terminal cancer or some chronic disease to be cured through faith in God's healing power? Hopefully, the following three contrasting testimonies will enlighten us and perhaps resonate with our experience and observation of life.

Barbara Cuminskey—When God Says "Yes"

The December 16, 1983 edition of *Christianity Today* tells the story of Barbara Cuminskey. By age 19, doctors had diagnosed her as having multiple sclerosis (MS), a degenerative disease that attacks the central nervous system, hardening tissues in the brain and/or spinal cord. She frequently became bedridden, but from 1972 to 1974 she was healthy enough to attend college as a handicapped student. After college she managed a job as a secretary; however, by 1977 her lung was paralyzing and she was constantly getting pneumonia and asthma. One lung collapsed. Her disease struck the bowels next, confirming Barbara's case to be the rare, severe MS that attacks the body's organs.

Breathing was so difficult that doctors did a tracheotomy. Her vision deteriorated to the point of technical blindness. Confined to bed, she spent nearly as much time in the hospital as out. There were several surgeries and three times she had respiratory and cardiac arrest. Tumors unrelated to MS grew on her hands and feet. Barbara was admitted as an out-patient at a nearby hospice. She was 31 and preparing to die. At age nine, Cuminskey had committed her young life to Jesus Christ. During her hospitalization a nurse would walk into her room and hear her talking to God as if he were a physical visitor. She was physically wrecked, but spiritually well.

"So came June 7, 1981. Days before, a local religious radio station mentioned Barbara's plight and suggested it for prayer.... On this summer day, a Sunday, Barbara sat in bed as two women from her church read cards to her. Barbara (but not the other two women) heard a voice over her shoulder: "My child, get up and walk." Barbara assumed it was God.... She told the two women she was going to walk and that they should alert her family. Since she had not walked in two years, the two women were confused. But they left the room.

"Barbara could not wait for her parents. She jumped out of bed. Elated, she started down the hall, where her mother met her. Barbara's legs, atrophied from lack of exercise, now had muscle tone and firmness. Her mother's first words were a shout: 'Calves! You have calves!' Her father grabbed his daughter and danced around the...room with her. After waltzing with her father,

Barbara did ballet steps, standing on her toes, leaping and laughing." (1)

Cuminskey's severe form of MS is medically incurable and her doctors admit she should have never gotten well. Her caved-in lung was restored to healthy functioning and her incurable chronic lung disease disappeared, as did the hand and feet tumors. The ileostomy and tracheotomy were reversed. Health was entirely restored, instantaneously. (2)

I have no reason to question the integrity of this inspiring story in one of the most highly respected Christian magazines in the world. In keeping with the two conditions I earlier mentioned for healing (faith and God's will), Barbara and her Christian supporters obviously prayed 'in faith', with a God-generated confidence in his desire to heal her, the inference being the request for healing was according to God's will. We would all like to see this type of miraculous healing of a serious physical disease as a common occurrence. The kingdom of heaven has arrived in Jesus! Be healed…and presto, it happens! But the biblical evidence we explored earlier and Christian experience, such as the next testimony, tell us that this is not a realistic hope for the present manifestation of kingdom of heaven on earth.

David Watson—When God Says "No"

On January 5, 1983, British Anglican author and renewal preacher, David Watson, discovered he had colon cancer. Watson immediately contacted a number of praying Christian friends for support, including John Wimber, then pastor of a large, charismatic church in California with the reputation of having one of the most impressive faith healing ministries in the world. Wimber informed David that he did not accept this cancer, and that he believed God wanted to heal David. He called the 4,000-member church to fasting and urgent praying for David's healing. Though the surgery removed the malignant section, he was informed that the cancer had spread to his liver. Doctors told him he could expect to live about a year. He felt devastated.

Wimber and two others who were also involved in healing ministries flew from California to visit David and pray for his healing. They "laid hands on" him, praying and rebuking the cancer in the name of Jesus Christ. David felt God was at work within his body and the next day testified to feeling vastly better. Wimber and his two friends remained for two more days of intensive prayer. Before returning to California, he said to David: "I believe that the root of [the cancer] has been cut and soon it will begin to die." (3)

In spite of the prayers of faith healers and thousands of Christians around the world; in spite of fourteen healing Eucharists conducted for him throughout England; in spite of special anointings with oil by Anglican priests and his own belief that God was healing him, Watson died peacefully on February 18, 1984, approximately thirteen months after the initial diagnosis of colon cancer. He was 50 years old. In his forward to Watson's book, *Fear No Evil*, J. I Packer reflected: "David's theology led him to believe right to the end that God wanted to heal his body. Mine leads me rather to say that God evidently wanted David home, and healed his whole person by taking him to glory in the way that he will one day heal us all. Health and life...are not what we die out of, but what we die into." (4)

Joni Eareckson Tada—When God Says, "My Grace Is Sufficient"

The vibrant and athletic Joni Eareckson (later Joni Eareckson Tada) became a quadriplegic in 1967, the result of a diving accident. She subsequently authored over 50 books. Her book, *Joni*, chronicles her battle to accept her handicap, how she struggled to overcome bitterness, despair and depression. In *A Step Further*, she dealt with the enigma of pain and suffering and shared some of the answers she found for her own situation.

In *Choices and Changes*, she relates the three significant choices she made in the previous ten years (1978-1988): playing herself in the movie, *Joni*; leaving the security of family and friends in Maryland to launch in California a new ministry to the disabled called Joni and Friends; and marrying Ken Tada, a high school teacher and coach. In *When God Weeps*, Joni explores in depth with co-author Stephen Estes why our sufferings matter to God and how, when we co-operate with him, they can deepen our friendship with him and mature the soul. (We will re-visit Joni's experience in more detail later.)

Reflections

Barbara Cuminskey was miraculously delivered from MS, a rare occurrence indeed. She went on to become a nurse and to lead a relatively ordinary life. David Watson passionately believed in

God's power to heal his cancer-stricken body and was the recipient of the faith and prayers of thousands of other Christians who just as fervently believed in God's healing power for him. David died just thirteen months after his initial surgery for colon cancer. His account of his faith journey and struggle to understand why cancer had afflicted him as told in *Fear No Evil* is nevertheless an inspiring testimony for anyone facing a similar predicament.

Early in her struggle with being a quadriplegic, Joni Eareckson Tada had prayed for miraculous deliverance from her condition. God denied her request. However, he empowered her creatively and purposefully to use her situation to minister effectively to thousands of people through her books, movie, and through her *Joni and Friends* ministry to the disabled. She has used her wheelchair for more than 40 years as a launching pad for a vital ministry of spiritual healing to scores of hurting people. Though her physical abilities were impaired, her spiritual potential was dramatically enhanced. From the perspective of eternity and the fruit of her life's ministry, was not Joni's spiritual healing more important than having her limbs restored to normal functioning?

These testimonies each reflect a slice of the reality of life. Of these three people, only Barbara Cuminskey experienced a miraculous healing in the sense of having her physical ailment permanently cured. But David Watson's reflections on what God was saying to him through his ordeal and the realization that not even death could separate him from the love of God became a profound inner healing for him. Death became his ultimate healing as he entered the more immediate presence of Christ (Philippians 1:20-26). Joni Eareckson Tada's experience of the grace of God through decades of confinement to a wheel chair reflects a spiritual healing with the kind of powerful impact upon others through her various ministries that most healthy Christians will never have. Did God choose not to heal her physically because he knew she would bear much more fruit for him through her disabilities than without them?

Dying Well

Our culture swamps us with media articles, television programs and advertisements about *living well* through special exercise programs, different diets and smart financial investments. How often do we hear or read anything about *dying well* (forgive the oxymoron)—other than encouraging people to plan ahead for their funeral expenses with a particular company? Are we increasingly becoming a death denying society that needs to learn how to die well? The sobering reality is that our lives are all terminal. The exciting truth of the Christian faith is that we can stare down death, challenging it as Paul did: "Where O death is your victory?...Thanks be to God! He gives us the victory through our Lord Jesus Christ" (1 Corinthians 15:55, 57). Hallelujah!

Dr. Paul Brand tells the inspiring story of Mrs. Savararyan, wife of the general superintendent of the hospital at Vellore, India, where he served as a surgeon: "Mrs. Savararyan...was a...saintly woman...[who] developed cancer of the breast, which quickly... metastasized into her lungs and throughout her body. Her doctors presented the terminal prognosis...and described the toxic effects of chemotherapy treatments, which would offer only palliative help.

"Mrs. Savararyan decided against prolonged treatment. 'Even if I have only a week or month to live, I want to live it awake and fully alive and conscious of the presence of God and his family,' she announced...Those...who visited [her] said, 'We did so to comfort her, but in truth we went to receive her overflowing comfort and strength.' As her pain increased, her spiritual strength also increased.

"I last saw Mrs. Savararyan early in the morning on Good Friday.... On the way to the church I stopped by her room.... She was as peaceful and courageous and inspiring as ever.... Within an hour...she died....

"I broke the news to the congregation from the pulpit.... The impact of her death...was electrifying.... I told the audience that I knew she had committed her spirit to the Lord...and that her final passing was but an instance in which she shook off her mortality. Her spirit...had been in God's hands long before death.... The same spirit that had already risen above pain and fear and all the problems that normally attend death had simply come to that moment when she said, 'Lord, into thy hands I commend my spirit.'

"...Mrs. Savararyan was not healed, not in the sense of her disease disappearing. But every person in that audience...knew that we had seen a miracle of profound dimension. Strength, patience, courage, hope, love—these too are the stuff in which God fashions miracles of healing." (5)

Mrs. Savararyan's death reminds me of Catherine Booth, co-founder, with her husband, William, of The Salvation Army. While dying from breast cancer she triumphantly proclaimed to her family from her death bed: "The waters are rising, but so am I. I am not going under, but over. Do not be concerned about your dying; only go on living well and the dying will take care of itself." (6)

The Apostle Paul also left us an inspiring testimony of dying well that, hopefully, we all want to emulate: "I am already being poured out like a drink offering, and the time has come for my departure. I have fought the good fight, I have finished the race. I have kept the faith. Now there is in store for me the crown of righteousness, which the Lord, the righteous judge, will award to me on that day—and not only to me, but to all who have longed for his appearing" (2 Timothy 4:6-8).

Our goal, as Christians, must certainly be to learn how to live and die well. There may be occasions when we feel compelled to pray for God's intervention for a life-threatening disease, either for ourselves or for someone else. Our merciful, loving God may grant our heart's desire. After a while, however, it may become obvious that God's will is to let nature takes its course. Then we will need to decide how to deal with the inevitable outcome, hopefully choosing to use the remaining time to let our family and friends see how the gracious presence of Jesus Christ can enable us to not only live well, but to also die well.

Discussion Questions

1. Regarding Barbara Cuminskey, David Watson, Joni Eareckson and Mrs. Savararyan: a. What were some of your thoughts and feelings as you read these three stories? b. Which one do you most identify with and why? c. How have

these examples affected your perspective on miraculous healing?

2. Share a personal example of someone you felt handled their approaching death very well.

3. Do you find it easy or difficult to discuss the idea of dying well? Why or why not?

4. What do you think dying well would look like for you?

Chapter 7
Faith Healing Investigated

Although some people claim to have either been miraculously healed or know someone who has experienced God's direct involvement in healing, it is difficult to find scientific or medical documentation that verifies such claims. Evidence is usually through personal testimony. In 1979 the Christian Medical fellowship of Great Britain published a booklet, *Some Thoughts on Faith Healing*. The editors, doctors Vincent Edmunds and C. Gordon Scorer, believe that God has the authority and power to perform a miracle at any time in his created world. The booklet contains the edited comments of their many professional colleagues and friends with whom they met to discuss the subject of faith healing. They acknowledge that being healthy means being free from disease mentally and physically, but focus their attention on the healing of the physical body.

Knowing the word 'miracle' can be overused to describe almost anything out of the ordinary, Edmunds and Scorer carefully define a miracle as "a rare and wholly inexplicable event. It should indicate an occurrence outside the course of ordinary human experience and not simply be applied to something which is uncommon." (1) (This definition would certainly encompass the healing ministry of Jesus.) Regarding physical healing, they limit the word *miraculous* to healing of diseases of various bodily organs where the disorder can be seen, shown on an X-ray plate, or a section of the unhealthy tissue can be examined. They assert: "When clearly observable *organic* (i.e. physical) conditions are present, it is easier to attain some basis of comparison between the usual results of medical treatment and instances where there is a claim [of] faith healing." (2)

They reviewed reported cases of miraculous healing throughout church history and concluded that *confirmed* cases of divine healing of physical diseases after the Apostolic Age (30-100 AD) are rare. In 1956 the British Medical Association replied to a series of questions put to it by the Archbishop of Canterbury's Commission on Divine Healing. The twelve doctors and nurses on the commission reported in 1958 that their extensive research lead them to conclude that patients suffering from emotional or psychological disorders may be 'cured' by various methods of spiritual healing just as they are by other forms of psychological treatment, but found "no evidence that *organic* diseases are cured solely by such means." (3)

Claimed Cases of Miraculous Healing

Some Thoughts on Faith Healing relates several individual examples of claimed miraculous healing through prayer. One case is about Margery Steven of Wimborne, Dorset, England, who reportedly recovered from a severe form of multiple sclerosis.

She testified: "I felt a warm glow go over my body. My left foot, which was doubled up, straightened out; my right foot, the toes of which were pointed to my heel, came back into position." (4) She then stood up and began to walk again. In a moment, her previously diseased, closed eye opened and she could see. Edmunds and Scorer state that this woman nevertheless at periods has not been free from symptoms, but understandably thanks God for her recovery from her previously disabled condition.

Edmunds and Scorer also reported cases of faith healing of a brain tumor, a compound fracture of the pelvis, viral meningo-encephalomyelitis and epilepsy. Their conclusion? The evidence of God's intervention in healing was often complicated by the involved patients usually having also been medically treated. Accurately determining whether God had intervened apart from medical treatment was therefore compromised. In short, reports of instant healings without medical intervention are not normally documented and thus are difficult to confirm.

Edmunds and Scorer note that in 1976 Professor John Dundee presented a paper entitled "Miraculous Healing" at a meeting of the Christian Medical Fellowship of Great Britain. Dundee had been able to investigate the cases of 32 patients who had clearly benefited from contact with a healing community called the Centre for Christian Renewal. One male patient had been diagnosed with bone cancer and had returned from Australia to die in Northern Ireland. He was carried to a healing service on a stretcher. During the night he heard a voice saying, "Get up and walk," which he did. His pain disappeared. He returned to Australia and was reported to be enjoying a healthy life.

Dundee encountered only one undesirable incident from this healing community. A middle-aged woman racked with pain from breast and bone cancer seemingly miraculously recovered following prayer and the laying on of hands. She subsequently testified about her cure and spoke at many healing services. Six months later her health rapidly deteriorated and she died. Her death upset many people because it put into question whether God had cured her.

"As a result of this survey I would commend, rather than criticize, the role of the church in healing the whole person," concludes Dundee. "I failed to find undisputed evidence of miraculous healing, but I did meet patients who were improved in mind and spirit. The doctor, in the providence of God, can help the body, the psychiatrist can help the mind, and I believe in the concept that the mind can affect the actions of the body in this life and the fate of the soul eternally. The ministry of the church...can play a major part in the healing of the whole [person]. Have we forgotten E.L. Trudeau's concept of what a good doctor should be able to do—'Cure sometimes, relieve often, comfort always?' With increasing knowledge we concentrate on cures and less on symptomatic relief. We almost completely ignore comfort. The church can place its priorities in reverse order—comfort, relief and cure. Working together, the ministrations of doctor and counselor will be complementary." (5)

Professor Dundee said he "failed to find undisputed evidence of miraculous healing." Yet, he tells of an Australian man diagnosed with bone cancer who went home to Ireland to die, but who recovered completely after attending a healing service and hearing a voice say, "Get up and walk." I'm puzzled why he doesn't view this as "undisputed evidence of miraculous healing?" Are we to assume he questions whether the man's diagnosis of having bone cancer was accurate? Or, does he think that the man's bone cancer is in remission but may return, thus suggesting his healing was not miraculous but the result of the medical treatments he received?

On his web site, *Is There a God?*, Australian Eric Hatfield presents more extensive and seemingly more definitive examples of miraculous healing than Edmunds and Scorer. He focuses on testimonies from American medical physician and researcher Dr. H. Richard Casdorph's book, *The Miracles*. In the mid-1970s Casdorph interviewed 10 people who claimed to have been miraculously healed of serious conditions. He analyzed the patients' X-rays and medical reports and also submitted them to specialists for review. Casdorph's book includes some of the X-rays. In each case, the medical facts showed that an extraordinary healing had taken place after the patient received prayer for healing. Here are three of the 10 documented cases Hatfield quoted from Casdorph's book.

Lisa Larios

"Lisa Larios was diagnosed with cancer of the hip when she was twelve.... Her family decided chemotherapy was too traumatic and called it off after one dose.... A friend invited them to a Christian healing service conducted by evangelist Kathryn Kuhlman. The friend fasted and prayed for a week beforehand.

"During the service, Lisa felt a warm feeling in her stomach, and Kathryn Kuhlman said someone in her section of the auditorium was being healed from cancer and should stand up. Lisa...stood up and was able to walk without pain for the first time since the problem had appeared. Lisa was X-rayed several times after that.... Something strange had indeed occurred. Further X-rays were taken and reviewed by several doctors, showing that Lisa's hip had been fully restored and the cancer was gone."

Marie Rosenberger

"In 1970, at age 44, Marie Rosenberger started suffering from severe headaches. She underwent brain surgery and a tumour was removed, but the surgeons could not remove it all, and the biopsy showed it was malignant. The tumour began to grow back, and Marie was not expected to live. The family decided to spend an evening praying for her healing and her husband stayed up all night. He had a vision of the tumour being healed, but Marie seemed little improved when she woke. However, she stopped taking her medication, and continued to improve, as visits to her neurosurgeon confirmed, with some amazement, until she was healed."

Marvin Bird

"Marvin Bird, a victim of arteriosclerotic heart disease, had his first heart attack at age forty-six, and over the next sixteen years was hospitalized seventeen times because of his condition. One artery was completely blocked and the others were half blocked, but he declined a coronary artery bypass because, at age 60, he didn't think he would survive surgery. He attended a healing meeting even though he wasn't then a believer, and an assistant, believing he had been healed, invited him to stand up. He couldn't previously do this on his own, but now was able to. Doctors later confirmed he was fully healed, and Marvin started to attend church and believe in Jesus." (6) Casdorph's other seven examples follow the same pattern.

Hatfield offers the following observations on Casdorph's 10 documented healings: "Ten people, all prayed for by Christians who believe in divine healing, all healed. That is surely enough to make any open minded person think. At the very least, we can say that something quite unusual happened in each case. Coincidence? The odds seem against it. Poor diagnosis? Ditto. Lies? The documentation suggests not. Real miracles? It seems likely!" (7)

Hatfield concludes: 1. "There is good documented medical evidence of unusual recoveries after prayer for healing. This evidence has been reviewed by medical specialists. 2. The probability of natural remissions seems remote, and the most believable explanation is surely that these were indeed cases of divine healing. 3. In many cases, people prayed for some time before the healing occurred. We should be encouraged to pray when loved ones need healing. They may not receive the healing, but it is possible that they may." (8)

Though Joni Eareckson Tada prayed for years to be delivered from her paralysis and wheel chair, God did not heal her. Yet, she fervently believes that there are times when God miraculously cures. In *A Place of Healing*, she relates a remarkable healing story about one of her personal friends, a Christian woman who had a severe bone marrow disease. After doctors had exhausted all possible medical treatments, they informed her that death was inevitable. However, she and others prayed, and when her doctor later examined her, he was dumbfounded. The man was not a Christian, but after doing several blood tests he exclaimed: "There is no natural or medical explanation I can give. Your situation was beyond hope. All I can say is that this is a miracle." (9) Fifteen years later, Eareckson Tada's friend was still completely healthy. (10)

In summary, British doctors Vincent Edmunds and C. Gordon Scorer acknowledged that miraculous healings can occur, but seem guarded about such claims, saying the patients involved often had also received medical treatment. In his book, *The Miracles*, American medical physician and researcher, Dr. H. Richard Casdorph, testifies to many healings which he would categorize as miraculous. God did not answer Joni Eareckson Tada's prayer for physical healing. She nevertheless still believes that sometimes God heals miraculously, as evidenced by the healing story she tells about her friend who was facing certain death because of a severe bone marrow disease. These various attitudes towards miraculous healing probably reflect the differing views on this issue within the Christian community as a whole.

What do I believe about miraculous healing? As God's dearly loved children, we have every right to fervently petition him for healing. I believe that there are times when God heals miraculously, but such healings are uncommon. Jesus exhorts us to be persistent in our petitions (Luke 11:5-8); however, after a period of time, we may sense our heavenly Father expects us to surrender to the mystery of his will and purposes as Jesus did in Gethsemane: "My Father, if it is not possible for this cup [of suffering and death] to be taken away unless I drink it, may your will be done" (Matthew 26:42).

Discussion Questions

1. In *Some Thoughts on Faith Healing*, doctors Vincent Edmunds and C. Gordon Scorer define a miracle as "a rare and wholly inexplicable event. It should indicate an occurrence outside the course of ordinary human experience and not simply be applied to something which is uncommon."

    Have you or someone you know experienced the cure of a serious physical disease without any medical assistance or where medical treatments had failed? Discuss.

2. Mentioned above is the example of a middle-aged woman with breast and bone cancer who was seemingly miraculously healed following prayer. She subsequently testified about her cure at many healing services. Six months later she died. Do you think this lady was cured of cancer? Why or why not?

3. If it eventually turned out after a couple of years that the man supposedly cured of bone cancer by faith healing had died from that disease, do you believe that God had miraculously healed him the first time? Why or why not?

Chapter 8
The Source of All Healing

The previous chapter's investigation of modern day claims of miraculous healing suggests they are not easy to prove scientifically, primarily because cured individuals at some point had also benefited from normal medical interventions. However, there appear to be observable occasions of remarkable healings that can best be described as miraculous, the result of God's direct involvement. In everyday living, of course, we wisely use the God-given means of healing provided through skilled medical practitioners. Though we may not feel the need to pray for God's direct intervention for ordinary physical illnesses normally cured by regular medical services, many of us would probably cry out to God for deliverance from a life threatening disease or a life or death situation arising from a serious accident.

Our plea for supernatural healing might depend on our age or the age of the one we are praying for. For obvious reasons, we feel differently about praying for a miraculous cure for a terminally ill four-year old child and a eighty-four year old adult, even if we are the latter. Whatever the age, we pray for God's intervention because we believe that with him all things are possible (Luke

1:37), knowing at the same time that the healing of a particular individual might not be according to his will (1 John 5:14). Even though we know miraculous cures are rare, our hope is that in our case, God will respond positively to our heart's cry.

Healing—Compassionate Concern

What is the basis for hoping that God may grant our desperate request? First, "God is love" (1 John 4:16), and "God so loved the world that he gave..." (John 3:16). What world? A rebellious, hurting world. Broken relationships, damaged bodies and disturbed minds. Divine compassion motivated God to liberate a motley bunch of Israelites from oppressive slavery: "I have...seen the misery of my people in Egypt.... I am concerned about their suffering" (Exodus 3:7). Centuries later when Israel had become slaves in her own land, enslaved by idolatry, immorality and social injustice, the prophet Hosea, by his life and words, reminded them of God's enduring love for them: "When Israel was a child, I loved him, and out of Egypt I called my son.... I led them with cords of human kindness, with ties of love" (Hosea 11:1, 4). God's people confidently asserted during worship at the temple in Jerusalem: "The LORD is compassionate and gracious, slow to anger, abounding in love" (Psalm 103:8).

Eventually that Divine Love walked upon the earth in Jesus of Nazareth—God in human flesh. Jesus made God visible. "Filled with compassion" (Mark 1:40-42), he healed a man who, because of leprosy, was isolated from his family and normal society. Jesus healed him physically and socially. Mark also relates that when

Jesus saw a large crowd pressing to see him "he had compassion on them, because they were like sheep without a shepherd." So he fed them spiritually by "teaching them many things" (Mark 6:34). Sometime later another large crowd gathered around him. Because they had nothing to eat, Jesus told his disciples he had "compassion for these people" (Mark 8:1-2). Through a miracle he fed them physically.

Jesus wept at the graveside of his deceased friend, Lazarus (John 11:35), and over the city that, through spiritual blindness and rebellion against God, was rejecting peace and inviting bloodshed and destruction (Luke 19:41-44). Compassion took him to the unspeakable agony of the cross where "God was reconciling the world to himself in Christ," says Paul (2 Corinthians 5:19). So, why not expect God to sometimes miraculously heal a physical disease to demonstrate his incomparable love for his people?

Healing—Heaven on Earth

Secondly, we can be open to an occasional miraculous healing because God has truly inaugurated the kingdom of heaven on earth—phase one—the initial manifestation of his kingly reign. I. Howard Marshall explains that "Jesus' mighty works [were] the means of the restoration of God's rule in the world, removing pain and sickness and substituting health and well-being, curbing the unruly elements (Mark 4:39) and toppling Satan from his throne (Luke 9:1; 10:17-18; Matthew 12:28). Jesus regarded himself as setting men and women free from the power of Satan, both physical (Luke 13:16) and spiritual" (Luke 8:2). (1)

The Source of All Healing

Bible scholars interpret Jesus' healing miracles as foreshadows of his intention to one day completely heal his entire creation. In other words, *when Jesus healed someone he was providing a glimpse into the future complete redemption of our bodies,* and giving us a sign to remind us of the glorious resurrection life awaiting his followers when disease and death will be no more. Why then shouldn't miraculous physical healing still occasionally occur to validate the presence of the kingdom of heaven on earth now, reminding believers that what God has started—the renewal of creation—he will finish? When he does intervene we are dramatically reminded that "the heart of the Eternal is most wonderfully kind." (2)

It is natural for some to question God when one of these miraculous cures does happen: "Why did you step in to heal the Whites' dying child but allowed ours to die—in spite of our faith and persistent praying?" Why would God intervene in one hopeless situation and not another? That is a mystery we must leave to his infinite wisdom. Nonetheless, we can encourage ourselves with the reminder that death ushers every Christian and innocent child into the glorious presence of Christ, permanently healed of all pain and suffering (Philippians 1:21-23; 2 Corinthians 4:16-5:8). If we are alive when Jesus returns, he will transform our frail, mortal bodies into immortal spiritual bodies freed from all diseases and infirmities (1 Corinthians 15:42-57; I Thessalonians 4:13-18). Praise God!

Miraculous healing not only demonstrates God's love and anticipates the glorious age to come; it is also a faith booster that encourages Christians to persevere in hope for the coming

85

total healing of all sickness and the elimination of death itself (Revelation 21-22). The resurrection of Jesus is the greatest sign of that yet to be wonderful reality for all of Christ's followers: "Our present sufferings are not worth comparing with the glory that will be revealed in us.... The [physical] creation itself will be liberated from its bondage to decay and brought into the glorious freedom of the children of God" (Romans 8:18, 21; 1 Corinthians 15). The process of "making everything new" has actually begun: "If anyone is in Christ, he is a new creation; the old has gone, the new has come" (2 Corinthians 5:17). "He who was seated on the throne said, 'I am making everything new!...Write this down, for these words are trustworthy and true' " (Revelation 21:5).

Miraculous Healing As Evangelism

Thirdly, for God's evangelistic purposes, it is plausible that he would still sometimes miraculously heal today, as was the case of Marvin Baird quoted in the previous chapter. Jesus' miraculous healings were windows of opportunity to elicit faith in him as Lord and Saviour (John 20:30-31). Though God's primary means today of creating saving faith in Jesus is through the proclamation of the "word of truth" (James 1:18) and by the illuminating grace of the Holy Spirit (John 16:8), why wouldn't he still occasionally use healing for his evangelistic agenda?

I realize that Jesus' healings did not automatically awaken faith in all those who witnessed them. When he healed "a demon-possessed man who was blind and mute," most people present were "astonished" and wondered if this powerful miracle was a sign that Jesus was the long-awaited "Son of David," their Messiah (Matthew 12:21-22). On the other hand, the antagonistic Pharisees, feeling threatened by Jesus' authority, accused him of casting out demons through Beelzebub, the prince of demons" (Matthew 12:24)! Though miraculous healings do not irresistibly draw people to faith in Jesus (John 15:22-24), and the danger of sensationalism is always present, the Bible records that they confirmed the truth of the gospel message and generated saving faith in many people (Luke 17:11-19; 8:40-48; Mark 5:1-20; Acts 4:12-22; 5:12-16; 9:33-35; 13:4-12.)

We must, of course, avoid seeking signs or spectacular demonstrations of divine power for public display only, that is, without any redemptive content or purpose (Matthew 12:38-39; 16:1, 4; Luke 11:16; John 2:18; 4:48; John 6:30.) But that does not mean we should limit the freedom of God by assuming or even insisting that he will never miraculously heal today in order to now and then lead some people to experience his saving grace through faith in Jesus Christ. There is nothing in the Bible that would rule out that possibility.

Though God's main way today of creating saving faith and new birth in Jesus is through the proclamation of the "word of truth" (James 1:18) and by the illuminating grace of the Holy Spirit (John 16:8)—unaccompanied by miraculous physical healing—why wouldn't he nevertheless still occasionally use healing for his saving purpose? In that regard, Michael Green offers several situations in which we could legitimately expect God to miraculously heal apart from ordinary medical means: "Might not it especially be the case in circumstances where people do not have the Bible available in their language to enlighten them about the story of Jesus' coming 'to save his people from their sins' (Matthew 1:21)?

"Where medical knowledge is so advanced as it is in the West, where two thousand years of Christian evidences (not to mention the sacred Scriptures) abound to authenticate Jesus' claims to Messiahship, the conditions would appear to be lacking in which we might have a right to expect a miracle in the New Testament sense, though we cannot exclude the possibility. However, in missionary areas, where there is only a tiny church in a vast pagan stronghold, where there is a shortage of medical means, where there may be no translations of the Scriptures available or where the people are as yet illiterate, where, furthermore there are definite spiritual lessons to be reinforced by it - *there, on the fringes of gospel outreach, we have a situation in which we may expect to see God at work in miraculous ways today* (my emphasis). That he does so is attested by all the missionary societies working in primitive areas. But to suggest that [physical] healing and salvation are always and properly inseparable goes against the evidence of Scripture, history and experience." (3)

Believing God's Promises

Finally, we can expect God to sometimes miraculously heal because his Word invites us to pray for his intervention. In my previous discussion of James 5:14-16 in chapter five, I pointed out that the passage was not an unconditional promise for physical healing. However, by emphasizing the conditions of faith and especially the will of God for the individual, I left open the possibility of miraculous physical healing. The context in the Book of James is a local Christian fellowship where a believer is ill. The elders of the church, who represent the entire fellowship, are expected to anoint the sick person with oil and pray for his recovery.

Because of the interconnectedness of the spiritual and the physical dimensions of human life, the situation also called for the forgiveness of sins. Healing would not have been complete if the soul was left unhealed. When there is confession of sin and trust in God's pardoning grace, spiritual healing will always occur. Though we cannot command God to heal physically or presume upon his healing powers, we can still be open to the possibility that he will intervene in some circumstances when that is his will for a particular individual. At the same time, of course, we should never ignore the ordinary means of healing that God has provided through trained medical personnel.

God—The Source of All Healing

Once in a while we learn through the media of a family or church that allowed, for example, a child to die rather than seek medical help. They believed that the child would be healed solely through prayer and faith. This belief obviously reveals a failure to understand God's revealed plan for his broken creation—to heal it totally, but not all at once. Though God may directly intervene to cure a particular disease, it is not a common occurrence. For the elimination of all illness, we have to patiently wait for the return of Christ, when sickness, pain and death will be forever obliterated.

Refusing to seek professional medical attention when sick and hoping that faith alone will cure us, fails to recognize God as Creator of all of life and his calling us to partner with him in our human endeavors (Genesis 2:15), including in the treatment of our various ailments. "Every good and perfect gift is from above, coming down from the Father of the heavenly lights," declares James (1:17). Surely the healing care of professionally trained doctors is one of our Creator's good gifts.

The image of God in humankind has been distorted by sin, but not eliminated. The God who heals is Creator and Redeemer. Though we are not all God's children by redemption, all people are his children by creation. Gifted by God, our Creator, doctors and other related professionals—Christian and non-Christian—channel their medical knowledge, skills and compassion into the alleviation of human suffering. Also, God has built into human beings a powerful immune system that continuously heals us by destroying bacteria and toxins that would make us ill. Recognizing God as Creator of all of life, the Judeo-Christian heritage has always affirmed God's use of ordinary means, including doctors and medicines, to heal his people of their diseases. Though he heals primarily through human channels, it is no less his healing. *All healing, miraculous and ordinary, is a gift of God,* a truth abundantly clear in Scripture.

Sacraments of Health

Through the prophet Isaiah, God instructed King Hezekiah of ancient Judah to apply a poultice of figs to his boil. Isaiah did not

The Source of All Healing

exhort the king to believe for a miracle. The poultice worked (2 Kings 20:1-7). Isaiah lamented that his people's spiritual "wounds and welts and open sores" were not "cleansed or bandaged or soothed with oil" (Isaiah 1:6). Jeremiah's plea for a "balm" in Gilead to heal his people's spiritual wound implies the widespread use of a medical remedy for some types of physical wounds and illnesses (8:22). In Jesus' parable of the Good Samaritan, oil and wine were used to heal the wounds of the injured traveler (Luke 10:34). Paul encouraged his co-worker, Timothy, to use wine to alleviate his stomach ailment and "frequent illnesses" (1 Timothy 5:23).

Since biblical times we have made gigantic strides in the treatment of human illnesses. The use of means other than faith and prayer has always been sanctioned by God for the alleviation of human suffering. William Booth, the founder of The Salvation Army, summarizes well both aspects of healing: "If there be any virtue in medicine, it is by the power of God; and if there be any skill in a surgeon, it is given him by God, to be employed for others.... We ought always to sympathize with the sick, pray in faith for their recovery, and at the same time use all available and lawful means to check disease, relieve suffering and prolong life." (4)

In response to human illness and suffering, many Christian denominations have built and administered scores of hospitals and clinics in both the underdeveloped and developed worlds. Through their medical services millions of people have been cured of common and not-so-common diseases. Public hospitals, though not faith based, are likewise God's healing hands extended through the doctors, nurses and other skilled health care workers who serve in them. In recent years, naturopathic medicine, which blends modern scientific knowledge with traditional forms of medicine, has also become increasingly popular in treating human diseases. "The pastor, physician and chemicals are all instruments of healing," says Rodney Clapp. "Anointing oil and penicillin can both be sacraments of health." (5)

Discussion Questions

1. We can still expect God to occasionally intervene to miraculously heal a physical disease. Why do you agree or disagree with that statement? Discuss.

2. In what sense are all medical professionals God's hands of healing?

3. What would you say to a Christian who does not want to take a seriously sick loved one to a doctor because they believe that God will cure through their prayers and faith?

4. "In missionary areas, where there is only a tiny church in a vast pagan stronghold, where there is a shortage of medical means, where there may be no translations of the Scriptures available or where the people are as yet illiterate, where, furthermore there are definite spiritual lessons to be reinforced by it - there, on the fringes of gospel outreach, we have a situation in which we may expect to see God at work in miraculous ways today. That he does so is attested by all the missionary societies working in primitive areas." —Michael Green

If we accept Green's proposition, realizing secular Western society today is generally biblically illiterate, and some would say even increasingly pagan in its beliefs, values and behaviour, should we expect to see God working miraculously to further his evangelistic agenda? Discuss.

Chapter 9
How Does God Heal?

In biblically exploring miraculous healing, I have mentioned some of the means employed to treat illness: faith, praying (sometimes accompanied by the laying on of hands), using natural medical treatments such as drinking some wine moderately, applying a poultice to a boil and oil to wounds. Today, of course, we have professionally trained medical practitioners, complex diagnostic machines, sophisticated surgery techniques and powerful medicines to diagnose and treat our diseases and alleviate human suffering. But, what are the mechanisms in our bodies through which God's healing power operates? How does God actually heal our bodies? A response to this question requires a holistic approach to our understanding of human personhood.

The most satisfying insights I have discovered to these questions come from an article in *Christianity Today* by Dr. Paul Brand and Philip Yancey. Brand was a Christian doctor who pioneered surgical procedures for many years with leprosy patients in India. Seeing human beings as holistic unities, Brand suggests that we can better understand how God heals when we view healing from its three inseparable dimensions: physical, mental-directed and spiritual. Each one impacts the others.

Physical Self-Healing

Brand reminds us that God has created human beings with an immune system with powerful healing mechanisms that regularly destroy bacteria and toxins and usually prevent us from becoming ill. When he set a fracture, he merely joined two ends of bone properly. The body then had to lay down the calcium needed for them to rejoin. Likewise, he could not cut through any part of the body and then sew it up unless he could count on the body's cells healing the incisions. He says: "No one who has studied the mechanisms and worked with them every day, harnessing them, directing them and aiding them, can brush aside the wonder of physical healing that God has built into each one of us.... For each breakdown, there are hundreds of examples of microbes slaughtered before they could cause damage, of tuberculosis patches isolated in the lungs and of breast cancers strangled by the body's own defenses." (1)

Brand accepts the possibility of miraculous healings; however, he sees them as rare exceptions and as not the normal way in which God runs the world. His conviction is that "At the physical level [God] relies on mechanisms put in place with his original design of the DNA spiral.... Among the thousands of patients I have treated, I have never observed an unequivocal instance of [divine] intervention *in the physical realm*. Many were prayed for, many found healing, but not in ways that counteracted the laws governing physiology. No case I have personally treated would meet rigorous criteria for a supernatural miracle. I have reached a personal conclusion that…God does not normally interact directly at the organic level…. Healing normally operates in the mental and spiritual realms that can in turn galvanize the body's own [God-given] healing processes. (2) How thankful we should be for God's good gift of our body's self-healing, powerful immune system in keeping us healthy.

Mentally-directed Healing

Brand contends that God works primarily through the mind "to summon up new resources of healing in a person's body." (3) As evidence of the incredible power of the mind in affecting the rest of the body, he gives several examples documented by modern science. The mind can alleviate pain. Brand saw impressive evidence of pain control while serving in India, where Hindu holy men would walk on burning coals, sleep on nails and string themselves up on poles with ropes pulling on meat hooks through their backs. He notes that in the placebo effect, faith in simple sugar pills sometimes deceives the mind into believing that relief has arrived and the body reacts appropriately. "Through biofeedback [some] people can train themselves to…control blood pressure, heart rate, brain waves and even vary the temperatures in their hands by as much as 14 degrees Fahrenheit," says Brand. (4)

Researchers have discovered that the brain produces chemical neurotransmitters called endorphins, some of which are much more powerful than morphine in controlling pain and impacting body systems. *Brand feels it is very probable that this mental-directed healing is the mechanism that results in claims of healing from faith healing ministries.* "The suffering person may well focus hope and faith and trust to such a degree that the physical body responds with the recovery," says Brand. "The mind is a powerful force, and God can use it for his good purposes." (5)

I interpret what he is saying to mean that passionately praying for God to heal can activate our body's immune system at a higher than normal level, which results in the body's being able to maximize its immune resources to overcome the disease or illness.

Conduit for the Spirit

Mental choices can have drastic effects on our physical health, and spiritual ills affect mental attitudes and consequently our total well-being. The psalmist testified: "Blessed is the one whose transgressions are forgiven, whose sins are covered. Blessed is the one whose sin the LORD does not count against him and in whose spirit is no deceit. When I kept silent, my bones wasted away through my groaning all day long.... My strength was sapped as in the heat of summer" (Psalms 32:1-3, 4).

The author is saying that his initial refusal to admit and confess his wrongdoing to God affected him physically. Taking ownership for his transgressions and confessing them to God released him from guilt and restored him to full spiritual and physical health (Psalm 32:5). Similarly, most of us have likely experienced physical headaches of varying severity, and not because of anything organically wrong with our brains, but simply from extreme emotional pressure or stress.

The Christian's mind is to be an instrument for the Spirit. "Be transformed by the renewing of your mind," says Paul" (Romans 12:2). Brand contends that "[Through the Spirit] we have the potential for direct contact with the Creator of the universe, and [the Spirit's dwelling] in us...can have a dramatic impact on our overall health...When the mind is God-centered and the person is 'walking in the Spirit,' cells receive a new direction, are enhanced and the whole person functions best.... The Spirit uses the natural milieu—the mind, nerves and hormonal systems that control all cells—to accomplish his [healing] work. A true faith healer works in concert with, not in opposition to, these in-built processes." (6)

In physical self-healing, mental-directed healing and the healing resulting from being in-dwelt by the Holy Spirit, Brand attributes God as the ultimate source of the body's healing. What approach then does he recommend that the Christian community should take towards those who are ill? "Those who pray for the sick and suffering should first praise God for the remarkable physical agents of healing he designed," suggests Brand, "and then ask that God's special grace will take hold of the person and give him or her the ability to use those resources to their fullest advantage. The church can then fulfill its role as Christ's body by laying hands of healing on the one who needs faith and hope, and love and comfort." (7)

Brand has seen remarkable instances of genuine healing accomplished in this way. "People of God have overcome the effects of diseases in staggering 'unnatural' ways, all mediated through the instruments of body and mind under the control of the Spirit," he says. "Fellow Christians can offer real...help in this process of setting into motion the intrinsic powers of healing in a person controlled by God. This...focused healing, attainable in no other way, does not contradict natural laws. Rather, it fully exploits the design features built into the human body." (8)

Healing—A Holistic Approach

Life is precious and when threatened with a terminal illness the realization of our imminent death can be painfully hard to accept. We may be interested in only one type of healing: an instant cure through a miraculous, supernatural deliverance. But what happens when health continues to deteriorate, when a disease is terminal, or a paralysis is irreversible? For the non-Christian, God offers the healing of the soul, the inner peace that comes through confessing personal sin, becoming reconciled to God, and committing one's life to Jesus Christ as Lord and Saviour. This spiritual healing is available through repentance and faith in Jesus (John 3:16; Ephesians 2:8-9).

Christians down through the centuries testify that the Holy Spirit provides a healing of the mind and soul when facing a terminal illness. We experience a deep peace when we stop struggling and place our complete trust in Christ for whatever happens. Some of Christ's followers even reach the point where they embrace death joyfully, believing the words of the apostle Paul that "death...will [not] be able to separate us from the love of God" (Romans 8:38-39), that "to be away from the body [is to be] at home with the Lord" (2 Corinthians 5:8), and that "to live is Christ and to die is gain" (Philippians 1:21).

Acknowledging the interconnectedness of body, mind and spirit, the medical profession has begun to recognize that the best way to approach wellness is by treating the whole person—body, mind and spirit. Thankfully, hospital chaplaincy ministry is being increasingly seen as a vital part of patient care. Palliative care has also gained importance with many hospitals and hospices now providing special support not only for people who are dying, but also for their loved ones.

Discussion Questions

1. Dr. Paul Brand believes it is very probable that mental-directed healing is the mechanism that results in so many claims of healing from faith healing ministries. "The suffering person may well focus hope and faith and trust to such a degree that the physical body responds with the recovery," says Brand. Do you agree/disagree with Brand? Discuss.

2. "Those who pray for the sick and suffering should first praise God for the remarkable physical agents of healing he designed, and then ask that God's special grace will take hold of the person and give him or her the ability to use those resources to their fullest advantage," suggests Brand.

   "The church can then fulfill its role as Christ's body by laying hands of healing on the one who needs faith, and hope, and love and comfort." If you agree with Dr. Brand's suggestion, write out a prayer for: a. a sick Christian friend with a curable disease b. a sick Christian battling a terminal illness c. a non-Christian who has learned he/she has an incurable physical ailment that will eventually lead to his/her death

3. How do you think you would react if you were informed that you only had a few months to live?

Chapter 10
Ecstasy and Agony

Exploring miraculous healing in the Bible, investigating reports of some modern claims of such healings, and my own experience of life have led me to conclude that miraculous cures, that is, healings that completely exclude medical assistance, are rare. Why? Not because of inadequate faith, but because God has chosen to heal his creation in two phases. The kingdom of heaven partially arrived in the first coming of Jesus, focusing primarily on spiritual healing, specifically the healing of our relationship with God and with one another. Miraculous healing is therefore not available simply by praying for it. However, when Jesus returns to consummate his kingdom, he will completely heal his redeemed people and renew the entire cosmos (Romans 8:18-21).

Why didn't God choose to fix his damaged creation in one grand swoop The Bible doesn't explicitly answer that question, but 2 Peter 3:1-9 provides a plausible clue. Peter appears to be addressing Christians having to contend with scoffers who were arguing that the world had not really changed since Jesus' first coming. They were questioning whether he would ever return to judge the world and eliminate evil once and for all. "The Lord is not slow in keeping his promise [to return], as some understand slowness," Peter replies. "He is patient with you, not wanting anyone to perish, but everyone to come to repentance" (2 Peter 3:9). God loves the people he created in his image (Genesis 1:26-27; John 3:16)—in spite of our disobedience and our spiritual and moral failures. Before Jesus returns, he wants to populate the world with an indefinite number of spiritually renewed people (John 3:3) who will obediently live under his redemptive rule—an idea also expressed by the Apostle Paul.

Paul shares with the congregation in ancient Rome his disappointment that most Jews were not accepting Jesus Christ as Lord and Messiah (Romans 9:1-5; 10:1-3). However, his letdown gives way to hope when he declares that many Jews have experienced "a hardening in part until the full number of the Gentiles has come in" (Romans 11:25.) He seems to be saying that though most Jews are currently resisting salvation through faith in Jesus, many more will turn to Christ after a *certain number* of Gentiles are converted (Romans 11:11-12, 25-26). Only God knows what that number is, but for Jesus to return early would obviously greatly limit the population of his kingdom. The more people—Jews and Gentiles—who submit to God's kingly rule now, the more will inherit the new heaven and new earth when Christ returns to totally heal his creation (Romans 8:18-25; Revelation 21-22).

Awaiting Jesus' return is also an opportunity for his redeemed people to grow in holiness (2 Peter 3:11, 14), to increasingly become in character like Jesus and thus be better prepared for the life awaiting us in the new heaven and new earth (Romans 8:29; Revelation 21:1-4). In the meantime, God calls us to take care of his good creation (Genesis 2:15) and learn from him how to live fully in the world as it is (John 10:10). Learning to be thankful for God's numerous blessings, even in the midst of heartache and pain, is a significant step towards that goal, as reflected in Byron Jacobs' Facebook entry, March 19, 2015. Because of serious health problems, Byron and Mary Jacobs were forced to retire early from their vocation as ministers of the gospel in The Salvation Army. Bryon's weak heart limits his activities, but he is the primary caregiver for Mary, who has been afflicted with multiple sclerosis and whose mobility is restricted to a wheel chair. Shortly before his Facebook entry, Byron had to work through government and various health facilities to find an appropriate facility for his mother. He shared his reactions to that experience and gave me permission to include it here:

Today I Wept

"Dementia…What a terrible affliction. I had not experienced this disease's impact until my mother was recently diagnosed with it and then my seven siblings and I had to eventually admit her to a long term care facility. When the reality of our decision finally sank in, I wept uncontrollably. I subsequently found myself thinking many things, including the following reflections:

- If your mind is working clearly and you are able to think sober thoughts, think of precious moments that you have enjoyed and be thankful that you remember.

- If you have legs that work, wiggle your toes and marvel at the connection of brain power to toe power. Walk, run, jump, dance and enjoy the gift of every movement.

- If your fingers, hands and arms connect as they should, and if you can, point at the sunset or sunrise, shake someone's hand and look them in the eye and let them feel the beautiful connection that you share. Hug, hug long, and hug a lot those you love and enjoy the thought that you can know and feel love beyond measure.

- If your lungs are healthy and you can breathe without exhaustion, regard breath as a privilege. Be grateful that the air around you enters your lungs without hindrance, and live life to the full.

- If your heart beats regularly and without obstruction, let the music of every beat move you to realize that your blood circulates through countless arteries. Be awed that you are indeed "fearfully and wonderfully made" (Psalm 139:14).

- If you can see, enjoy the colors and scenery, the mountains and valleys, sunset and sunrise. Observe the smiles and tears and be moved again and again.

- If you can hear the simple movement of trees blowing in the wind, or the sounds of the mighty ocean, or the most incredible waterfalls, or if you can hear the sound of a sigh, savour these experiences.

"My life intermingles with people who cannot remember. Some cannot walk or hug and for others every breath is a struggle. Some need others to lead them where they cannot see to go. Some watch television and hope that words will appear so they can hear through the written word. Today I wept at the thought that mother is well into not remembering the simple and most important things. Though living in a broken world, I pray that God will help me to remember, to be hopeful and thankful so that I can be a blessing and encouragement to the people around me."

Choosing to cultivate a hopeful and grateful heart during the struggles of life is a powerful medicine for sustaining an optimistic attitude as we patiently wait for Jesus to return and totally heal his broken creation.

Sustaining Hope

A persistent physical ailment, caring for a loved one with dementia, or an ongoing battle with cancer can be discouraging and wear us down. We need resources to maintain a hopeful attitude under such circumstances. I believe strongly in the usual Christian prescription of daily communication with God when we pour out our hearts to him, downloading our frustrations and worries onto him and asking for the strength to persevere, and even trying to be a blessing to others during our trials. Daily reading God's Word for promises of comfort will reassure us of his love at a time when we might wonder if he really cares about us. Regular Sunday worship and fellowship with fellow Christians can be a tonic for our weary souls and an antidote for ingratitude. Listening to soul-stirring hymns can take our minds off ourselves, help us to be thankful for God's rich blessings, temporarily lift us to the heavenly realms and reassure us of the eternal hope of life with Christ after death.

It saddened me that my own mother's dementia reached the point where she could no longer coherently talk to me.

Interestingly though, when we wheeled her to the fellowship room at her nursing home for a sing-a-long of old Christian hymns, including songs about heaven, enough of her long term memory remained for her to join in the singing with a smile on her face. During her dying moments, my sister and I were with her in the private palliative care room of the nursing home. After taking her final breath, her strained face relaxed and I was surprised to see her lips briefly forming a smile. I wonder if she caught a glimpse of Jesus as her soul left her body, for "to be away from the body...[is] to be present with [Christ]," says the Apostle Paul (2 Corinthians 5:8).

In addition to the spiritual prescriptions listed above to sustain a hopeful attitude, I recommend a daily dose of reflection upon the numerous spiritual blessings we enjoy through our relationship with Jesus Christ our Saviour. The Apostle Paul wrote that though we were "dead in our sins and transgressions...gratifying the cravings of our sinful nature and following its desires and thoughts...God, who is rich in mercy, made us alive with Christ even when were dead in our transgressions [and]...raised us up with Christ and seated us with him in the heavenly realms in Christ Jesus" (Ephesians 2:1-6). Hallelujah!

Though formerly separate from Christ, we "have been brought near" through his atoning sacrifice (Ephesians 2:13). Though we have "all sinned and fall short of the glory of God, [we are] justified freely by his grace through the redemption that came by Jesus Christ" (Romans 3:23-24). Forgiven and clean, we need not be worried about God's condemnation or eternal judgment (Romans 8:1). We therefore "have peace with God through...Christ...and we rejoice in the hope of the glory of God" (Romans 5:1-2). Will that hope ever disappoint us? No, "because [God] has poured out his love into our hearts by the Holy Spirit, whom he has given us" (Romans 5:5).

In offering ourselves fully to God we "have been set free from sin and have become slaves to God, the benefit we reap leads to holiness, and the result is eternal life" (Romans 6:22). We have received "the Spirit of wisdom and revelation" to know Christ better (Ephesians 1:17). We are privileged as well to be "God's workmanship," his work of art, "created in Christ Jesus to do good works" (Ephesians 2:10). Awesome.

Living now in the first installment of the kingdom of heaven on earth also means that God gives us everything we need for life. "If God is for us, who can be against us? He who did not spare his own Son, but gave him up for us all—how will he not also... graciously give us all things" (Romans 8:31-32)? Our good and loving God has not promised to give us all we want, but he has promised to provide for all our needs, including the strength and grace to successfully cope with anything life throws at us. "My God will meet all your needs according to his glorious riches in Christ Jesus," says Paul (Philippians 4:19). Glory to God!

Jesus lived close to his heavenly Father and called him "Abba, Father," an intimate term that Jews would never use when referring to God (Romans 8:14-16). When we choose to follow Jesus, the Spirit of Jesus Christ, God's Son, enters our lives. With the Spirit of the Son indwelling us, we naturally feel close to God and call him Father as well. Paul further says that "The Spirit [of Jesus in our hearts] testifies with our spirit that we are God's children"

(Romans 8:16). Just as a good father loves his children, Jesus assures us that our heavenly Father loves us dearly and will take good care of us (Matthew 6:25-34). Wow.

He also tells us that the Holy Spirit is the down payment guaranteeing the glory that awaits every Christian beyond this life: "Now it is God who has made us for this very purpose and has given us the Spirit as a deposit, guaranteeing what is to come" (2 Corinthians 5:5). That assurance of life eternal with Jesus brings peace and comfort in life's struggles. God wants us to learn to live victoriously through our "present sufferings," knowing that we can be "more than conquerors through him who loved us" (Romans 8:18, 37). How wonderful to be a son or daughter of God through trusting in Jesus as our Saviour!

In addition to all of these wonderful spiritual blessings that we can enjoy as followers of Jesus Christ, how thankful we should also be for the many skilled people whom God uses to provide medical care when we are injured or become ill. Do we appreciate the effort, research time, money and trained personnel required to develop the powerful medicines, imaging machines, operating equipment and techniques used to diagnose and treat our ailments? What happens, for example, when a baby is born with a serious heart defect? At the appropriate time, a surgeon operates on the infant's heart and corrects the problem. The baby becomes a healthy child. Amazing. Are heart, lung, kidney and liver transplants so common now that we take them for granted, not appreciating them as God's good gifts in saving some people from certain death?

Do we truly appreciate the powerful healing mechanisms God has built into the human body, an immune system that daily destroys threatening germs without our even knowing it? Sometimes these invaders overwhelm our body's ability to kill them. We then access readily available medicines that come to our rescue, occasionally even saving us from death. God is good. How often even in our church prayer times do we thank God for the healing he provides through the excellent medical services from which we benefit?

Ecstasy and Agony

Though Jesus has inaugurated the kingdom of heaven on earth and we presently enjoy these many benefits of living under his redemptive reign, bad things can still happen to us. Paul reassures us, however, that "in all things God works for the good of those who love him, who have been called according to his purpose" (Romans 8:28). Paul is not saying that everything that happens to us is good. He means that with Christ now living in us, he can help us bring some good out of our painful experiences and situations. The main good that God wants to accomplish in us through these difficulties is "to conform us to the likeness of his Son, [Jesus]" (Romans 8:29).

Our tendency in trying times is to pray for a quick fix, but character development doesn't happen overnight. God wants us to co-operate with him so that the hardships of life purify and strengthen us, making us increasingly like Jesus now while also preparing us for the life to come. Personal holiness—becoming like Jesus—is a life-long journey. Sanctification, as this process is called theologically, requires our complete dedication to Jesus Christ and to his will and purpose for our lives: "I urge you, in view of God's mercy, to offer your bodies as living sacrifices.... Do not conform any longer to the pattern of this world, but be transformed by the renewing of your mind" (Romans 12:1-2). Abandoning ourselves to God becomes an exciting adventure that leads us eventually into his glorious presence.

Living in the tension between the present and future manifestations (already/not yet) of God's kingly rule means experiencing varying degrees of joy and agony. The delights of the honeymoon and the birth of a baby change to agony when a few years later the best medical care available cannot prevent the child from death by leukemia. After a period of pain-filled grieving, the parents eventually regain a joyful spirit—though they will never forget their beloved child. (Incidentally, having been a pastor for many years, I know that telling parents before they are emotionally ready, to "move on" or "get on with life", can be hurtful. We need to allow them whatever time they require to grieve and feel whole again.)

An athlete's exuberant celebration in winning an Olympic gold medal may turn to despair when a car accident lands him in a wheel chair for the rest of his life. The athlete eventually learns to successfully cope with his disability and may even flourish, including enthusiastically participating in competitive sports with other handicapped athletes. Another athlete in a similar accident may end up battling depression for many years and require ongoing medical attention. "We…who have the first fruits of the

Spirit, groan inwardly as we wait eagerly for…the redemption of our bodies" (Romans 8:23), says the Apostle Paul.

Even when healthy and strong, we know that eventually our bodies become weak and we die. There is no escaping death. Or is there? Jesus promised that "Whoever lives and believes in me will never die" (John 11:26). The Apostle Paul, who had a vision of the resurrected Christ on the Road to Damascus, declared: "If the Spirit of him who raised Jesus from the dead is living in you, he who raised Christ from the dead will also give life to your mortal bodies through his Spirit who lives in you"(Romans 8:11). Resurrection life awaits the followers of Jesus. Whatever life throws at us, we can still daily choose to appreciate and celebrate all of the physical and spiritual blessings God has made available to us in Christ. "To him be the glory forever" (Romans 11:36).

Discussion Questions

1. What have been some of the moments of ecstasy and agony in your life?

2. What gets you through the hard times?

3. Of all the blessings mentioned in this chapter—including the medical blessings—which ones do you most appreciate? Why?

4. What kinds of losses have you grieved over during your life? How do you feel that you have grown during those painful experiences?

Chapter 11
Increasing Our Capacity for God

In focusing on miraculous healing from physical diseases, it is easy to neglect the larger biblical picture of other kinds of suffering, especially the hardships experienced because of our faith in God. While Hebrews 11 is replete with the victories of some of the Old Testament saints, it also lists their many sufferings. Moses chose to be mistreated along with the people of God (Hebrews 11:24-25). Though "women received back their dead, raised to life again, others were tortured and refused to be released, so that they might gain a better resurrection" (Hebrews 11:35). In our usually safe and generally affluent way of life in the West, we can't imagine how we would react to the experiences mentioned in Hebrews 11:36-38: "Some faced jeers and flogging, while still others were chained and put in prison. They were stoned; they were sawed in two; they were put to death by the sword. They went about in sheepskins and goatskins, destitute, persecuted and mistreated. The whole world was not worthy of them."

Called to Suffer

The startling revelation of the Bible is that Jesus actually calls his people to suffer for and with him: "If anyone would come after me, he must deny himself and take up his cross daily and follow me" (Luke 9:23). If you were trudging along a road with a cross on your back in ancient Israel during the time of Jesus, no one would have assumed you were gathering wood for your fireplace. Everyone knew your destiny: You would be nailed to that cross. While Jesus was not saying that all those who choose to follow him would be affixed to a Roman gibbet to endure the brutal agony of physical crucifixion, he surely meant that following him would involve some pain.

Suffering—a Badge of Honor

When the resurrected Jesus commissioned the apostle Paul to be a servant of the gospel, he informed him through Ananias of how much he would have to "suffer for [Christ's] name" (Acts 9: 16). Paul later reminded the Christian assembly at Philippi that they had been called "to suffer for Christ" (Philippians 1:29). He told the Corinthian believers that "the sufferings of Christ flow over into our lives" (2 Corinthians 1:5). Paul and his evangelistic team confessed: "We must go through many hardships to enter the kingdom of God" (Acts 14:22). Because of his loyalty to Christ, Paul suffered floggings, several imprisonments, 39 lashes on five occasions, three separate beatings with rods, stoning once, three shipwrecks and a host of other hardships (2 Corinthians 11:23-33).

Jesus warned his disciples that insults, persecution and hatred for his sake are expected badges of honour: "Blessed are you when people insult you, persecute you and falsely say all kinds of evil against you because of me. Rejoice and be glad, because great is your reward in heaven" (Matthew 5:11-12.) Peter's encouragement to believers suffering unfairly because of their loyalty to Jesus Christ echoes the words of Jesus: "If you suffer for doing good and you endure it, this is commendable before God. To this you were called, because Christ suffered for you, leaving you an example that you should follow in his steps.... When they hurled their insults at [him] he did not retaliate; when he suffered he made no threats. Instead, he entrusted himself to him who judges fairly" (1 Peter 2:20-21, 23).

Purposeful Suffering—Beautifying The Soul

Are these kinds of sufferings meaningless? No, they are purposeful. They are for the sake of Christ and the advancement of his kingdom of "righteousness, peace and joy in the Holy Spirit" (Romans 14:17). What happens when opponents of the Christian faith observe followers of Christ bravely and positively embracing persecution and pain, demonstrating forgiveness and love instead of hatred and anger towards their enemies? Hopefully, some adversaries begin to think that what these Christians are saying about Jesus must be true and end up embracing the Christian faith themselves. I believe this is what happened in the case of Saul of Tarsus, the fierce Jewish persecutor of the infant church.

The closing verses of Acts 7 tell us that a frenzied mob rushed at Stephen, a Jewish convert to Jesus, and "dragged him out of the city and began to stone him. Meanwhile, the witnesses laid their clothes at the feet of a young man named Saul" (7:57-58). We can infer from verse 59 that Saul observes Stephen's courage in the face of death and witnesses his forgiving heart as he is being pelted by rocks and crying out: "Lord, do not hold this sin against them." He's sounding like Jesus on the cross: "Father, forgive them, for they don't know what they are doing" (Luke 23:34). Instead of calling out to God to back up his witness for Jesus by protecting him from harm or striking his opponents dead, Stephen prays for God to forgive them!

What kind of an impact did that have on Saul? Although "Saul began to destroy the church [and] dragged off men and women to prison" (Acts 8:3), surely the Spirit of God would use Stephen's bravery and forgiving attitude to begin to sow seeds of doubt in Saul about the rightness of his actions. He was likely wondering, "How could Stephen pray for God to forgive us? Could there be some truth in what he's been teaching about Jesus being Lord and Messiah?" I think God used Stephen's Christlike example of a forgiving spirit to prompt Saul (later called Paul) to re-evaluate his actions and prepare him for God's saving intervention on the Road to Damascus.

Western culture tends to glorify success and winning, often at any price. Weakness and failures are uncomfortably tolerated. Everything must always be getting better, from our health to the economy. "Faith is more than the power to change things for the better," testifies Ronald Dunn. "Oh, we would like to do that. But that isn't faith's greatest power.... Popular spirituality is power-based; everything is interpreted in terms of power.... In our attempt to win the world by impressing the world, we have abandoned the confrontational language of the cross for the wooing language of power, might, success and winning. The true power of our faith is power that the world calls weakness, and the victory of our faith is victory that the world calls failure.

"The Christ we follow was 'made perfect' through suffering" (Hebrews 2:10), continues Dunn. "We prefer to be made perfect through success. But grace will not do for us what it did not do for Christ—exempt us from suffering.... And so...*faith is not necessarily the power to make things the way we want them to be; it is the courage to face things as they are.*" (1) Dunn discovered by personal experience the bracing truths of which he speaks. A faithful pastor, he lost his manic-depressive son to suicide and for 10 long years struggled with depression himself.

Our culture conditions us to believe in instant gratification and immediate relief from any sort of pain or discomfort. How do we hear the text, "Endure hardship as discipline" (Hebrews 12:7)? Do we believe that "God disciplines us for our good, that we may share in his holiness" (Hebrews 12:10)? Have we forgotten that our maturing in character means more to God than our comfort? Do we believe that the purpose of hardship and discipline is to beautify the soul?

We spend billions yearly on over-the-counter medications, vitamins, supplements and various exercise programs to maintain or improve our health. We are living longer and healthier. Called to suffer for Christ? Have we embraced the Christian truth that

"God has not arranged everything on earth for our health and pleasure, but, rather, has arranged everything to stimulate the development of strong character, that sin, not pain, is the greatest evil, and growth in Christlikeness, not pleasure, is the supreme worth?" (2)

Much Suffering Can Be Redeemed

At some point in our lives we all have to face various types of pain and suffering: losing a spouse or a child in a car accident; coping with a parent's or spouse's deteriorating Alzheimer's disease; recovering from childhood sexual abuse; handling the pain of broken marriages and rebellious children; battling cancer; and absorbing the hurt of a rebellious child seduced by the drug culture. This is part of the fabric of life for many people, and they want to know if there is some temporal and even eternal purpose to their suffering. The good news is that with Christ's help much suffering can be redeemed by choosing to co-operate with him to bring some good out of it. That perspective requires a difficult choice, but is nevertheless an emotionally healing and empowering one.

Because Joni Eareckson Tada co-operated with God in using pain to mature her character, she testifies in her book, *A Place of Healing*, that her sufferings have deepened her experience of personal holiness. She writes: "A no answer [to my request for physical healing] has purged sin from my life, strengthened my commitment to [Christ], forced me to depend on grace, bound me with other believers, produced discernment, fostered sensitivity, disciplined my mind, taught me to spend my time wisely…and

Increasing Our Capacity for God

widened my world beyond what I would have ever dreamed had I never had that accident in 1967. My affliction has strengthened my hope, made me know Christ better, helped me long for truth, led me to repentance of sin, goaded me to give thanks in times of sorrow, increased my faith and strengthened my character. Being in this wheel chair has meant knowing [Christ] better, feeling his pleasure every day."(3)

Her personal testimony in dealing with being a quadriplegic reveals other profound insights. "When suffering forces us to our knees at the foot of Calvary, we die to self," she says. "We cannot kneel there long without releasing our pride and anger, unclasping our dreams and desires.... In exchange, God imparts power and implants new and lasting hope.... God reveals more of his love...power and peace as we hold fast the cross of suffering.... To believe in God in the midst of suffering is to empty myself; and to empty myself is to increase the capacity for God. *The greatest good suffering can do for me is to increase my capacity for God.*" (4)

She helpfully reminds us that "Our call to suffer comes from a God, tender beyond description. If we do not cling to this through life's worst, we will have missed everything and grow to hate him." (5) She adds: "God does ask his children...to suffer (Luke 9:23). Only two places...are exempt—a few areas in Southern California, and a few in Florida, run by a friendly talking mouse who wears suspenders.... Yet, by sharing Christ's sufferings [we taste] the power of his resurrection.... We will thank God endlessly in Heaven for the trials he sent us here. This is not Disneyland—it is truth." (6) I agree with all of these profound truths; however, I must admit that it is tremendously challenging to live them.

Exposing the Poison of Sin

Some of Joni Eareckson Tada's perceptive spiritual insights may be unpleasant medicine to swallow, but we would be wise to acknowledge that all truth is ultimately healing. "Our pain, poverty and broken hearts are not [God's] ultimate focus," she writes. "He cares about them, but they are merely symptoms of the real problem. God cares most—not about making us comfortable—but about teaching us to hate our sins, grow up spiritually and love him. To do this, he gives us salvation benefits only gradually.... He lets us continue to feel much of sin's sting while we're headed for Heaven. This constantly reminds us of what were being delivered from, exposing sin for the poison it is. Thus evil (suffering) is turned on its head to defeat evil—all to the praise of God's wisdom." (7) She would agree with Augustine's observation that "God judged it better to bring good out of evil, than to suffer no evil to exist." (8)

I appreciate Eareckson Tada's deep and spiritually challenging insights regarding personal pain and suffering. I want to add, however, that victims of atrocities and terrible suffering first need to experience empathetic listening ears and compassionate hearts to move forward in finding any good in or bringing any good out of their unspeakable pain. A gang-raped woman would find it impossible to see any purpose in such a vicious act—at least in the short term. In the longer term, if she brings her brokenness to Jesus Christ and experiences his healing grace, she may devote herself to conveying empathy and comfort to other rape victims. In spite of professional counseling and/or a substantial healing through faith in Christ, other similar victims may struggle with depression for many years.

Increasing Our Capacity for God

As I write these words the news media are reporting on massively destructive earthquakes in Nepal that have killed over 8,000 people. Can any of us see any good coming out of that disastrous calamity and heartbreaking tragedy? Probably not much—at least not yet. (It is encouraging to see so many nations uniting to help this struggling country recover from this catastrophe.) Our not being able to see any good in these cases does not mean that our all-knowing God sees no potential for good in them. Our knowledge is limited; God's knowledge isn't.

If miraculous physical healing and protection from human tragedies were the birthright of every Christian in this life, would not many people convert to Christ only out of self-interest, providing security against the sicknesses and disasters that afflict the rest of humankind? In particular, miraculous healing for all would eliminate the opportunity for the deep spiritual growth that can occur through hardship and pain. Taken to its logical conclusion, if miraculous physical healing were available to everyone simply through faith, it would eliminate all diseases and death, thus ushering in the kingdom of heaven in all its fullness and glory now. But this cannot happen because the New Testament reveals that the removal of all sin, evil and suffering—the total renewal of all of creation—awaits the return of Jesus, the timing of which only our heavenly Father knows (Acts 1:7).

The Sanctification of Wounds Incurable

On rare occasions, through prayer and faith in God, healing may be demonstrated in a miraculous deliverance from some physical ailment. When the desired physical healing does not occur, the good news is that we can still experience the deeper healing—the spiritual healing of the soul. Embracing our pain, accepting the reality of a non-cure in this life, is a kind of healing in itself—especially when we allow it to beautify our souls in conforming us to the character of Jesus Christ, and thus also preparing us for the next life.

Nicky Gumbel relates a story told by Gavin Reid, former Bishop of Maidstone, England. In Reid's congregation was a boy who had severely injured his back falling down the stairs when he was a year old, resulting in being frequently hospitalized. When Reid interviewed him in church, the boy said "God is fair"—even though he had spent 13 of his 17 years in hospital. When Reid asked him if he truly thought that was fair, the boy answered, "God's got all of eternity to make it up to me." (9)

The final goal of the Christian life is not to reach 90 years of age without ever experiencing any form of intense hardship or suffering, but to become increasingly like Jesus. In the end, God will make it up to every faithful sufferer. Could P.T. Forsyth be right in saying that too often so much of our energy is "engrossed with healing or preventing pain, that it is withdrawn from the noble enduring of it, from the conversion and sanctification of wounds incurable?" (10)

Discussion Questions

1. "Popular spirituality is power-based; everything is interpreted in terms of power.... In our attempt to win the world

by impressing the world, we have abandoned the confrontational language of the cross for the wooing language of power, might, success and winning." Why do you agree or disagree with Ronald Dunn's statement?

2. "God has not arranged everything on earth for our health and pleasure, but, rather, has arranged everything to stimulate the development of strong character, that sin, not pain, is the greatest evil, and growth in Christlikeness, not pleasure, is the supreme worth." To what extent do you think Christians and people generally live that truth expressed by Joni Eareckson Tada and Steve Estes?

Chapter 12
God's Pain

When we are in tune with God, the healing truth that keeps a melody in our hearts, even in life's darkest moments, is expressed in the song that many of us learned in Sunday school: "Jesus loves me, this I know for the Bible tells me so." Persistent hardships and ongoing pain can, however, tempt us to question the goodness and love of God. Does he really care about *me*? I invite you to imagine this scenario: You are driving through your home city when your local radio station reports that a mother and her child were found brutally murdered an hour ago. You may find yourself saying out loud, "Oh God, how awful. How sad." Some time later you learn that it is the Browns, a family that attends your church and the husband and wife participate in your bowling league. Your feeling of sadness likely increases.

Suppose, on the other hand, that the news report is not about the Browns. As you draw near to your house, you see four parked police cars and an ambulance with their lights flashing. You discover that the two viciously killed people mentioned on the news are your beloved wife and precious five-year-old child! Now, how would you feel? Horror and grief beyond description. Anger and rage might also consume you—at least initially. You weep profusely.

Does God Understand Our Pain?

Why is the third reaction much more intense than the others? The murdered woman and child are the two people you love more than anything or anyone else in the world. Your pain is far more acute now because you love your wife and child so deeply. The pain of grief is the price we pay because of our capacity to love and establish close relationships. God is progressively revealed in the Bible as a God of incalculable love: "God so loved the world that he gave his one and only Son." (John.3:16). Paul says that in the suffering of the cross "God was reconciling the world to himself in Christ, not counting [our] sins against us" (2 Corinthians 5:19). This means that in the suffering of Jesus, the Son, the Father also suffered—just as we suffer when our children suffer.

John tells us that "God is love" (1 John 4:16), meaning that God's essence is self-giving, sacrificial love. Christ's cross reveals that pain is the price God paid and continues to pay because of his infinite capacity to love us—a comforting truth for us to reflect upon when confronted by human suffering. Why? Because knowing God's pain means we have someone who understands our pain. Initially overwhelmed by acutely painful emotions, we may accusingly wag our finger at God, saying, "You don't care. You don't know what I'm going through." However, later reflections upon the cross of Christ prompts us to acknowledge that he does know; he does care. Many would testify that this truth is mysteriously comforting and healing.

Blaming God for life's ills does not lessen personal or human suffering generally. A more constructive attitude is required. Many sufferers down through the centuries have experienced relief from their distress through prayerfully reading the Old Testament Book of Psalms, particularly the complaint and lament psalms that demonstrate how people individually and as a community of faith expressed their pain. They experienced comfort and healing by unloading their anger and bewilderment onto God: "How long, O LORD? Will you forget me forever? How long will you hide your face from me? How long must I wrestle with my thoughts and every day have sorrow in my heart?...But I trust in your unfailing love; my heart rejoices in your salvation. I will sing to the Lord for he has been good to me" (Psalm 13:1-2, 5-6). In God's presence lament turns into a renewed confidence in God's love and kindness. Honesty with God about how we feel is a healing medicine for the soul.

It is therapeutically wise to bare our hurting hearts to God; however, to become and remain whole emotionally and spiritually we must also avoid inflicting pain upon others, and do whatever we can to alleviate human suffering. How much better our world would be if more people took to heart Albert Einstein's sobering observation that "the world is too dangerous to live in—not because of people who do evil, but because of people who sit and let it happen." (1)

The Ultimate Discovery

In *Every Day With Jesus*, Selwyn Hughes quotes Augustine as saying that "the answer to the mystery of the universe is God and the answer to the mystery of God is Jesus Christ." (2) Hughes himself further suggests that "The answer to the mystery of Christ is…his sacrificial spirit, the supreme evidence of which is the cross." (3) Hughes calls this the ultimate discovery: "The cross spells out the message that God is prepared to take into himself the suffering caused by sin and, indeed, to take onto himself the very sins of the ones he created. No other religion…conceives of such a thing…. Through [the cross] we see that *at the centre of the universe is redeeming love*. No greater discovery could be made or will be made than that—on earth or in Heaven. It is the ultimate in discoveries." (4)

Hughes felt that the world's religious leaders stumble over this profound truth. He quotes a leading Muslim who said during a television debate that "A God who would stoop and suffer is not perfect." And a Hindu commented: "If Brahman would suffer he would be unhappy, and if he were unhappy, he would be imperfect, and if he were imperfect he would not be God." (5) The amazing revelation of the Bible is that God passionately loves his people and thus suffers with and for us.

The Gain of Pain

Before he created us, God knew we would rebel against his sovereignty and bring untold miseries upon ourselves, including death, and bring grief to his own heart. Why then did he create us? Because in his infinite wisdom and incomparable love he knew that the glorious gain would be worth the pain. What was the gain? Christ's sufferings for his people were redemptively purposeful in making salvation (eternal life) available to the world. When we accept this wonderful gift and our attitudes and hearts are changed by God's transforming grace, we are able to be a blessing and comfort to others. "Just as our Lord's wounds give him a special empathy for us in our struggles and sorrows, so our wounds can be used to soothe and strengthen those who hurt," writes Selwyn Hughes in *Jesus the Wounded Saviour*. "The more we have suffered, the more our suffering can speak to others. My own battle with prostate cancer over ten years has brought me to moments of despondency. I do not pretend to be a warrior when it comes to illness, but I am aware that in the…darkest moments there is always a stream of strengthening…power that flows from God…. I have felt a resurrection power supporting me for which there can be no other explanation than that God is at work." (6)

God's Crazy Love

Brennan Manning tells how in the winter of 1968-69 he chose to live in a cave in the mountains of the Paragosa Desert in Spain. In the little chapel section of the cave hung a cross with a carved figure of Jesus on it. In gazing upon that image one night, he says he heard in faith Jesus say: "For love of you I left my Father's side. I came to you who ran from me, who did not want to hear my name. For love of you I was covered with spit, punched, beaten and affixed to the wood of the cross…." 'I figuratively saw the blood streaming from every pore of his body and heard the cry of his wounds: "This isn't a joke. It is not a laughing matter to me that I have loved you." 'The longer I looked, the more I realized that no man has ever loved me…as he did. I went out of the cave, stood on the precipice and shouted into the darkness: Jesus, are you crazy? Are you out of your mind to have loved me so much?'" (7)

In an online meditation, *Healing The Broken Heart*, Ted Schroder relates a touching story about Pastor David Biebel. "Biebel's firstborn son, Jonathan, died in early childhood from a bizarre neurological disease," relates Schroder. "In a poem entitled, *Lament*, Biebel asks, 'Destroy! Destroy! Our little boy, what sad, demented mind, unkind would dare? God?'

"When his second son was diagnosed with the same illness," continues Schroder, "David dared to articulate what he was actually feeling: 'If that's the way it's going to be, then God can go to hell.'

"They were honest words, but they tasted like blasphemy…. As he drove to his parents' home…to tell them Christopher too was afflicted with the illness that took Jonathan's life, Biebel realized the ironic truth of his 'blasphemous' words, and with that realization came God's comfort. On Good Friday God…did go to hell. As David sobbed, he sensed God's message to him: 'I understand, my son…. I've felt your pain and carried your sorrows. I know your words arose from guilty grief beyond control, and I love you still and always will.' " (8)

"To understand the cross is to understand God," comments Timothy Sanford. "To stare at the cross is to get the clearest, deepest look into the heart of God. God's crazy love shines through every splinter of the cross. It's strange.... It's scary. It's God's heart, a heart broken to death, not killed by a Roman spear. I can't look at the cross without it screaming out, 'I love you!'" (9)

God's passionate love for us overcame his utter distaste of our sinfulness. In the cross of Jesus God's love absorbed the pain of our sin and transformed it into forgiveness and reconciliation. With God's help our pain can also be redemptive. We can choose to become better or we can choose to become bitter. Our pain can soften our hearts, drawn us closer to God, and deepen our empathy for and service to others who are suffering. "Praise be to the God and Father of our Lord Jesus Christ, the Father of compassion and the God of all comfort, who comforts us in all our troubles, so that we can comfort those in any trouble with the comfort that we ourselves have received from God" (2 Corinthians 1:3-4), exclaims the Apostle Paul.

Graham Kendrick's song, *For This I Have Jesus,* brings consolation to countless people because it reflects these truths about the cross of Christ, that the wounded but resurrected Jesus is present with us in our pain and brokenness:

> For the joys and for the sorrows,
> the best and worst of times,
> for this moment, for tomorrow,
> for all that lies behind;
> fears that crowd around me,
> for the failure of my plans,
> for the dreams of all I hope to be
> the truth of what I am:

For this I have Jesus,
for this I have Jesus
for this I have Jesus, I have Jesus.

For the tears that flow in secret,
in the broken times,
for the moments of elation,
or the troubled mind;
for all the disappointments,
or the sting of old regrets,
all my prayers and longings,
that seem unanswered yet:

For the weakness of my body,
the burdens of each day,
for the nights of doubt and worry
when sleep has fled away;
Needing reassurance
and the will to start again,
a steely-eyed endurance,
the strength to fight and win: (10)

Seeing God's Back

These insights into the meaning of the cross of Christ, of God's identification with suffering humanity, help us to better appreciate his unwavering love for us. They do not, of course, give us a complete understanding of God and his ways in the world. When Moses was having second thoughts about whether he was capable of leading his people into the Promised Land, he asked God: "Now show me your glory" (Exodus 33:18). He must have felt that knowing God totally, experiencing God in the fullness of his being, would empower him to overcome the challenges ahead. God's response? "I will cause all my goodness to pass in front of you, and I will proclaim my name, the LORD, in your presence. I will have mercy on whom I will have mercy, and I will have compassion on whom I will have compassion. But...you cannot see my face, for no one may see me and live.... There is a place near me where you may stand on a rock. When my glory passes by, I will put you in a cleft in the rock and cover you with my hand until I have passed by. Then I will remove my hand and *you will see my back; but my face must not be seen*" (Exodus 33:19-23).

What's the difference between seeing God's face and seeing his back? Figuratively, the text is contrasting the difference between a full and a partial revelation or manifestation of God's being. As a mere mortal, Moses could never fully *see* or understand God. The most important thing he needed to experience about God is that he is merciful and compassionately loving and could therefore be trusted for the future. That revelation eventually sustained Moses through the perilous days ahead, including leading his people through their 40 years of wilderness wanderings. The even deeper revelation of God's suffering love revealed in the cross of Jesus reassures us even more of his perfect goodness and of our need to trust him when pain and suffering threaten to overwhelm us.

Though we can know God intimately, he is ultimately elusive. We cannot control him. If we could understand God totally, he would not be God. When doubts or questions about God's nature or about human injustice and suffering have surfaced in my own life, I have found comfort in Deuteronomy 29:29: "The secret things belong to the LORD our God, but the things *revealed* belong to us and to our children forever; *that we may follow all the words of the law*." In spite of some mysteries about life and God, his Word reveals enough to enable us to love and serve him and his people, and thus to please and glorify him.

Is there a better alternative approach to the question of suffering and evil generally than that provided by the Christian faith? Atheism? Believing there is no God removes the question about his goodness and power in creating a world with the potential for so much heartache and pain. It does not, however, solve the problem of or provide a more satisfying explanation for the existence of evil or suffering in all its forms.

Most suffering is initiated by humans who choose to inflict it upon their fellow human beings. Could God have created creatures without that freedom? Yes. But they would be robots without any capacity to choose to love and enjoy relational closeness and the other joys of life. If we choose to believe in a perfectly good, all-knowing and all-powerful Creator, then we can accept by faith Augustine's insight quoted earlier that "God judged it better to bring good out of evil, than to suffer no evil to exist." God judged it better to bring good out of pain, than to prevent it from occurring.

The World We Want Is Coming

Earthquakes, tornadoes, wars and other calamities along with human diseases and suffering continue, but the drama of redemption is unfolding. Jesus' first coming inaugurated the kingdom of heaven on earth with its countless blessings. Living under the kingly, redemptive reign of Jesus Christ, his followers must dwell not on the pain and heartaches of life, but on the many benefits that flow *now* from his suffering, death, resurrection and gift of his Spirit.

Timothy Keller had a man in his first parish who had lost his eyesight after he was shot in the face during a drug deal. The man had been extremely selfish and cruel, and had always blamed his constant legal and relational problems on others. The loss of his sight had devastated him, but had also deeply humbled him. "As my physical eyes were closed, my spiritual eyes were opened," he told Keller.... I finally saw how I'd been treating people. I changed, and now for the first time...I have friends, real friends. It was a terrible price to pay, and yet...it was worth it. I finally have what makes life worthwhile." (11)

In the present manifestation of the unfolding drama of redemption, God "has [already] blessed us in the heavenly realms with every spiritual blessing" (Ephesians 1:3). We are, however, still anticipating and waiting for the finale. Then we will finally celebrate the elimination of all sin and suffering and enjoy forever the presence of the One who has promised to make everything new (Revelation 21:4). In the meantime, we long for creation's total healing. "We groan inwardly as we wait eagerly for the redemption of our bodies, for in this hope we were saved, " says the Apostle Paul. "But hope that is seen is no hope at all. Who hopes for what he already has? But if we hope for what we do not yet have, we wait for it patiently" (Romans 8:23-25).

"The Bible tells us that God did not originally make the world to have disease, hunger and death," writes Timothy Keller. "Jesus has come to redeem where it is wrong and heal the world where it is broken. His miracles are just not proofs that he has power but [are] also wonderful foretastes of what he is going to do with that power. Jesus' miracles are not just a challenge to our minds, but a promise to our hearts, that the world we all want is coming." (12)

Can God cure every disease? Yes. Will God cure every disease? Yes, but not now. However, because "the world we all want is coming," we wait patiently and with the hopeful attitude expressed by George Matheson:

> O Joy who seekest me through pain,
> I cannot close my heart to Thee;
> I trace the rainbow through the rain
> And feel the promise is not vain,
> That morn shall tearless be. (13)

"Amen. Come Lord Jesus" (Revelation 22:20)!

Questions

1. "Through the cross we see that at the centre of the universe is redeeming love." Share an experience when you doubted that truth or powerfully experienced it.

2. In the troubles and pain of life, what brings you the most comfort? How have you grown through these experiences?

3. Discuss Albert Einstein's observation: "The world is too dangerous to live in—not because of people who do evil, but because of people who sit and let it happen."

Endnotes

Chapter 1: Looking For Answers

(1) Joni Eareckson Tada, *A Place of Healing*, (Colorado Springs, Colorado: David C. Cook Publishing, 2010), p. 15.

Chapter 2: Miracles—Signs With a Purpose

(1) Craig L. Blomberg, *Baker' s Evangelical Dictionary of Biblical Theology*, ed. Walter A. Elwell, 1996, www.biblestudytools.com/dictionaries/bakers-evangelical-dictionary/miracle.html.

Chapter 4: Heaven on Earth

(1) O. Hofius, "Miracle," *The New International Dictionary of New Testament Theology*, vol. 2, ed. Colin Brown, (Exeter, Devon: England, The Paternoster Press, 1976), p. 631.

(2) Victor Shepherd, *Our Evangelical Faith*, (Toronto: Clements Publishing, 2006), pp. 40-41.

(3) Walter W. Wessell, "Mark," *The Expositors Bible Commentary*, vol. 8, (Grand Rapids: Zondervan Publishing House, 1984), p. 629.

(4) Ibid., p. 629.

(5) Ibid. p. 629.

(6) Joni Eareckson Tada and Steven Estes, *When God Weeps*, (Grand Rapids: Zondervan Publishing House, 1997), p. 63.

(7) Menzie Nicola, *CP Church and Ministry*, "Snake-Handling W. Va. Pastor Dies After Poisonous Bite During Sunday Service," www.christianpost.com/news/snake-handling-w-va-pastor-dies-after-poisonous-bite-during-sunday-service-75769.

(8) *Life Application Study Bible, New Living Translation*, (Wheaton: Tyndale House Publishers, 2004), p. 1,665.

(9) G.E. Ladd, *A Theology of The New Testament*, (Grand Rapids, Michigan: Wm. B. Eerdmans Publishing Company, 1974), pp. 76-77.

(10) Ibid., p. 76.

(11) Ibid., p. 77.

Chapter 5: The Evangelistic Impact of Miraculous Healings

(1) G.W.H. Lampe, *Miracles: Cambridge Studies in Their Philosophy and History*, "Miracles In The Acts of The Apostles," ed. C.F.D. Moule, (London: A.R. Mowbray and Company Ltd., 1965), p. 171.

(2) Paul Brand with Philip Yancey, "A Surgeon's View of Divine Healing," www.christianitytoday.com/ct/2003/julyweb-only/7-7-43.0.html. Originally printed in *Christianity Today*, November 1983.

(3) D. A. Carson, "Matthew," *The Expositors Bible Commentary*, Vol. 8, ed. Frank E. Gaebelein, (Grand Rapids: Zondervan Publishing House, 1984), p. 207.

Chapter 6: Yes, No, My Grace Is Sufficient

(1) Rodney Clapp, "Faith Healing: A Look At What's Happening," *Christianity Today*, December 16, 1983, pp. 16-17.

(2) Ibid., pp. 16, 17.

(3) David Watson, *Fear No Evil*, (London: Hodder and Stoughton, 1984), p. 57.

Endnotes

(4) Ibid., p. 7.

(5) The story about Mrs. Savararyan and the material for chapter nine are adapted from Paul Brand and Philip Yancey's article, "A Surgeon's View of Divine Healing," *Christianity Today*, November 1983. Later reproduced in *Prayer: Does It Make Any difference?* Copyright 2006 by Philip Yancey. Quotations are from the web reprint: www.christianitytoday.com/ct/2003/julyweb-only/7-7-43.0.html. Used by permission.

(6) Allen Saterlee, *Notable Quotables*, (Atlanta, Georgia: The Salvation Army Supplies, 1985), p. 49.

Chapter 7: Faith Healings Investigated

(1) Vincent Edmunds and C. Gordon Scorer, *Some Thoughts on Faith Healing*, (London: Christian Medical Fellowship, 1979), p. 10.

(2) Ibid., p. 10.

(3) Ibid., p. 59.

(4) Ibid., p. 66.

(5) Ibid., p. 81.

(6) Eric Hatfield, *Is There a God?* www.is-there-a-god.info/life/tenhealings.shtml.

(7) Ibid.

(8) Ibid.

(9) Joni Eareckson Tada, *A Place of Healing*, p. 76.

(10) Ibid., p. 77.

Chapter 8: The Source of All Healing

(1) I. Howard Marshall, "Jesus in the Gospels," *Expositors Bible Commentary*, vol. 1, (Grand Rapids: Zondervan Publishing House, 1979), p. 529.

(2) Fredrick W. Faber, "Souls of Men, Why Will Ye Scatter," verse 3; Oratory Hymns, 1854, www.hymnary.org/text/souls_of_men_why_will_ye_scatter.

(3) Michael Green, *The Meaning of Salvation*, (London: Hodder and Stoughton Ltd., 1965), pp. 224-225.

(4) William Booth, *Faith Healing: A Memorandum*, (London: The Salvation Army, 1902), pp. 64-65.

(5) Rodney Clapp, "Faith Healing: A Look At What's Happening," *Christianity Today*, December 16, 1983, p.15.

Chapter 9: How Does God Heal?

(1) Paul Brand with Philip Yancey, "A Surgeon's View of Divine Healing" www.christianitytoday.com/ct/2003/julyweb-only/7-7-43.0.html.

(2) Ibid.

(3) Ibid.

(4) Ibid.

(5) Ibid.

(6) Ibid.

(7) Ibid.

(8) Ibid.

Chapter 11: Increasing Our Capacity for God

(1) Ronald Dunn, *When Heaven Is Silent*, (Milton Keys, England: Word Books, Nelson Word Ltd., 1994), pp. 43-44, 46.

Endnotes

(2) Joni Eareckson Tada and Steven Estes, *When God Weeps*, (Grand Rapids: Zondervan Publishing House, 1997), p. 117. Used by permission of Zondervan. www.zondervan.com. All rights reserved.

(3) Joni Eareckson Tada, *A Place of Healing*, (Colorado Springs, Colorado: David C. Cook Publishing, 2010), pp. 55-56.

(4) Tada and Estes, *When God Weeps*, pp. 136-137.

(5) Ibid., p. 40.

(6) Ibid., p. 65.

(7) Ibid., p. 56.

(8) Augustine of Hippo, en.wikiquote.org/wiki/Augustine_of_Hippo. .

(9) Nicky Gumbel, *Searching Issues*, (Lottbridge Drove, Eastbourne, England: Kingsway Publications, 2001 edition), p. 19.

(10) Rodney Clapp, quoting P.T. Forsyth in *Christianity Today*, Dec. 16, 1983, p 17.

Chapter 12: God's Pain

(1) Dean L. Overman, *A Case for the Existence of God*, (Lanham, Maryland: Rowman & Littlefield Publishers, Inc., 2009), p. 99.

(2) Selwyn Hughes, *Every Day With Jesus-One Year Devotional, Light for the Path*, (Farnham, UK: Crusade for World Revival, 1999), Day 41.

(3) Ibid., day 41.

(4) Ibid., day 45.

(5) Ibid., day 45.

(6) Selwyn Hughes, *Jesus the Wounded Saviour*, (Farnham, Surrey, UK: Crusade for World Revival, 2006), pp. 76, 77, 65-66.

(7) Brennan Manning, *The Signature of Jesus*, Revised edition, (Sisters, Oregon: Multnomah Books, Questar Publishers, 1996), pp. 42-43.

(8) Ted Schroder, *Healing The Broken Heart*, quoting Dr. Diane Comp from her book, *A Window to Heaven: When Children See Life In Death*, listserv.virtueonline.org/pipermail/virtueonline_listserv.virtueonline.org/2012-March/013156.html.

(9) Timothy Sanford, "Cross Purposes," *Discipleship Journal* 110 (March/April 1999), p. 56.

(10) Graham Kendrick, "For This I Have Jesus," www.grahamkendrick.co.uk/songs/item/26-for-this-i-have-jesus-for-the-joys-and-for-the-sorrows.

(11) Timothy Keller, *The Reason for God*, (New York: Riverhead Books, Penguin Group, 2009), p. 25.

(12) Ibid., p. 99.

(13) George Matheson, library.timelesstruths.org/music/O_Love_That_Will_Not_Let_Me_Go.